The

Phillips - Martindale

Family Histories

By John Eacott

This work is the effort of John Eacott
and Donna Eacott, nee **Phillips**

Helpful contributions were made by Karen Parkhill, Nancy Reynolds, Richardt Phillips, Gerald Sanders and others.

ISBN 978-0-9878227-8-9

Permission to use extracts can be made from John Eacott at Eacott@execulink.com The book may be ordered from www.lulu.com

Owners of this book may request a pdf file copy for research purposes.

My web sites are eacott.info and eacott.weebly.com

This book is dedicated to our grand children
Nathan, Mackenzie, Tessa and Aven

Phillips

and

Martindale

These stories are about the families who came to Ontario from England. The Phillips came from the Dartmoor area of Devon and the Martindales from Lancashire. Included in passing are Tanners and Fairhurst and other connected families.

In this work I have attempted to gather the details of lives and stories about the relatives of my wife and her family so they may better understand their own personal histories. I have used online and historical notes to create this book. As different descendent lines enlarge I have taken the story from the earliest days found to the children and some grandchildren of all the discovered families. I have left spaces so notes may be added for other people to include other details.

The genealogy records are not completed for every generation, particularly past the 3rd as the data was not known. As more becomes known updates can be created.

As this work is printed on demand, it is possible to update the contents with additional material. Contributions for revisions are welcome.

I hope the readers find this book to be interesting and to help the readers understand who they are.

Everyone who has lived deserves recognition.

John Eacott
Curries Ontario
June 2021

Version 1.1

The Phillips Ancestry Story

This is a story of one Phillips family. It attempts to tell of the life of **William Phillips** and his children who left Devonshire England and came to Canada. Today the descendants are numbered in the 5th to possibly the 8th generation and bear many different surnames but each person could genetically trace back to William. In this story we start you on your discovery of William and his children. Perhaps you can add more!

There are many gaps in these lives lived. In researching the old documents and handed down information, errors were discovered about who was who and when. Even with what I have learned I can not always be certain but I have done my best to show what I know and how I know it.

William Phillips was born in Devonshire England about 1798/9

It would be nice to be able to identify his parents and grandparents but there is not enough evidence at this time. But we do know a lot about this William who is the earliest proven ancestor of this Phillips family tree. Actually he was correctly known as William Philips and lived at Dury farm.

The Phillips or Philips or Philps name in the 1841 census of England appears in the southwest of England, Devon, Cornwall, Somerset, Dorset and Gloucestershire. The next few pages show possibilities but not proof of his parentage. Read on and see why.

The William Phillips who came to Oxford County Ontario in about 1853 could have been one of several possible persons but I am pretty certain for reasons that will be told that he has been properly identified.

William Phillips was reputed to have been born in Lydford (also Lidford) parish Devon about 1799. There is no birth or marriage record for him at Lydford. Lydford parish was the largest parish in all of England and it contained all of Dartmoor Forest. It also was very sparsely populated. Lydford extended South almost to Tavistock and Cornwood and east to Widecombe in the Moor. As a result the people living in this parish had to endure a long travel to go to the Lydford church for baptisms, weddings and funerals. There were no proper roads on the moor but there were tracks or trails. As early as the 1200's people were allowed to take their dead to other nearby parishes for burial because of the problem of transporting the dead to

Lydford for burial. Widecombe on the Moor was the most frequently chosen church but there were others. Tavistock, Peter Tavy and Cornwood were other parishes abutting Dartmoor and Lydford parish.

Dartmoor was not actually a forest but a barren rocky upland area and since about 1200AD it was controlled/owned by the Duke of Cornwall who is also the Prince of Wales, the eldest son of the monarch of the day.

Cornwood is a village and parish directly south of Dartmoor. A William Philips was born in Cornwood parish and baptized April 19, 1798. He was the son of William Philips and Elizabeth. His father was a mason. Could they have lived at Dury farm?

Then on Nov 15, 1799 another baby William was baptized by William and Anne Philipps. William was also a mason and also at Cornwood. This infant was likely baptized within a week or two of birth.

But wait, there is more! Four couples, all Philips: William and Jenny, William and Jane, William and Anne and William and Elizabeth are all listed as (stone) masons and all at Cornwood and all had children in the 1790's. There were in addition to the two Williams: John, Roger, Susannah, and Robert. Other than John none of those names are replicated in our William Phillips family. This poses a problem about the tracing of a tree backwards. Who might be the correct parents if this is our family? Is the family line descended from Elizabeth or Anne? Did baby William and Elizabeth die and William the father then marry Anne and sire another William? We can only speculate.

Who were these William Philips who were (stone) masons? The moors were mined for granite stone used in making stone houses and there were large mines or pits between Cornwood and Peter Tavy. So these people, cousins, fathers and sons, all had the same trade at least on the baptism records.

Another William Phillips was baptized 26 May 1799 at Saint Sidwell church, Exeter, father William, mother Elizabeth. They did not leave Exeter so the family line continues there to this day as shown by census records. This is not our William.

Another William Phillips was born at Bampton, Devon and became a saddler in London. His ancestry traces back to the 1600's and he was quite successful in his trade but his children did not have names that matched William of

Lydford. This is not our William.

Another William Phillips was born to Thomas Soldier Phillips at Tiverton July 1, 1797. That location would make one wonder how William got to live in the moor. He is probably not our William.

It must also be considered that there were other William Phillips born in the southwest of England.

Phillips is a fairly common name. In the United States there are 2 million in the census records, 232 000 immigration and passenger records. They come from several countries. However with the information that the ancestor William was born in the late 1700's in England, we can narrow the possibilities down considerably.

The first meaningful census in England was in 1841. Before that church baptism records were the usual and almost the only way to identify a person's existence.

It is clearly shown in the census of 1841 that a William Phillips lived in Lydford (Lidford) parish. He and his family lived at Dury farm and he is definitely the ancestor of this family tree because we can trace back person to person. That is because all the children's names and years of birth are reported there. We can't specifically identify his parents. However as he claims to have been born in 1798/9 and there is a William born that year to **William and Anne Philips of Cornwood,** we might think these may be his parents but more proof would be needed.

But in the 1851 census William says he was born in Tavistock in 1798. Was this a generalization or was he quite specific? Because in 1851 **Richard Philips**, possibly his father, in his 80's was living in Tavistock as a widowed lodger and in 1841, Richard in his mid 70's was living with Roger, presumably his son who possibly was William's brother, age 35 wife Elizabeth 34 and their children Richard 15, Mary 13, William 11, James 6, John 4, and Thomas 1. These names by co-incidence happen to be almost the same names William and his wife Elizabeth gave to their slightly younger children at Dury. Roger and family lived at Trear Cottage near Black Brook which appears to be a row house a few miles west from Dury farm on the only road towards Tavistock . William names his first son Richard, so is his father this Richard?

William in 1841 lived near Postbridge, deep in the moor, and Lydford was a particularly inconvenient church to reach from Dury farm. In fact until 1782 there was no road at all across the moor. The road built then went from Tavistock to Widecombe through Postbridge.

The Phillips name was known around the western edges of Dartmoor. A number of Phillips, Philips, Philip, families lived in the 1700's in Lydford, Tavistock, Peter Tavy, Cornwood and other places. How related they were is not known. How they spelt their names is not especially important because spelling was not nearly as fixed as it is today. One detail that can be important is the record of the given names to children. These tend to be passed down from generation to generation.

Dury farm is in the next parish a few miles directly north of Cornwood. An adult William shows up there in the first census in 1841. He names his first son Richard and second son William. None of his children are named Thomas which disassociates him from Thomas Soldier Phillips who was born 1797. Yet the year of birth is also sometimes something not well recalled. There will be many examples in the material that follows that show recalled ages are often out several years in their reporting.

In trying to locate who might be a grandparent, registers from parishes around Dartmoor were examined. As William was born 1799 we need to look for a father born 20 to 40 years earlier or roughly 1760 to 1780 and also a grandfather born before 1755. Men at that time seldom married young as they needed to be able to provide for their family.

There were a few William Philips born in Plymouth some miles to the south. William was born 1775 to William and Rebecca; William born 1755 to Thomas; Willliam 1719 born to William and Mary; William 1710 born to William and Mary and in 1695 William born to William and Joan. It would be a wild guess to connect any of these to this family.

The other Philips born were not William. So let's go back to Richard.

Richard Philips was born at Peter Tavy in 1767 and lived in nearby Tavistock in 1851. Peter Tavy is a hamlet and parish next to Dartmoor. It is about 20 km from Dury. Our William lived more or less in the middle of the moor. Richard had a son Roger living in 1841 near Peter Tavy. Roger could easily be William's brother.

Yet it is recorded in Lydford parish records that Richard lived in Lydford parish near Peter Tavy not in that parish. Perhaps he lived out on the moor as did Roger. If you lived in a parish, you were expected to go to the parish church to be baptized, married and buried.

Since William named his first born Richard we can assume there was a good reason such as being named after father or grandfather.

Another Roger and Elizabeth Philips lived in Lydford Village in 1824 when they baptized son Thomas and in 1826 Jane Geak. Later at Summerhill in the parish there were other baptisms John 1829 and Tamsin 1833. This is a different Roger than the aforementioned.

There were other, older Philips in the Lydford register. In 1721 Valentine Philips married Mary Powel. Earlier in 1712 Roger and Tamsin Phillips baptized William Priggens Phillips and Roger and Margaret Phillips baptized a daughter Jane in 1707.

In 1751 **Richard Philips married Sarah Chub**, both gave Peter Tavy as their location although they were married at Lydford. Soon John was born to them. **Later in 1764 William was born to Richard and Sarah. This William could be the father of our William or Richard 1767 could be.** I say this because names and location and time are 3 important factors in deciding who is who.

Let's now look at other possible parents and grandparents. Earlier a Richard Philips was born in 1737 to Richard and Mary; however, in 1751 he would have been only 14.

In 1778 Richard Philips of Peter Tavy was buried at Lydford. Would this be the father of Richard born 1767? Other Philips were identified with the Peter Tavy area: Samuel was buried in 1777, Elizabeth was buried in 1764.

Not identified specifically with the Peter Tavy area, as there was no real reason to always do so, is the baptism of Roger in 1731 son of Richard and in 1737 Richard junior son of Richard and Mary at Lydford. And even earlier Richard and Mary baptized daughter Mary in 1732.

Other earlier Lydford parish Philips were Valentine Philips who married Mary Powel in 1721 and had several children. He died in 1749. Roger and Tamsin baptized William Piggins Phillips in 1712, and Roger and Margaret Phillips baptized Jane in 1707. Also appearing at Lydford were Henry and Elizabeth with children from 1761.

A Roger was born at Mary Tavy (near PeterTavy) in 1790 and moved into Lydford by 1851; At Ermington , John son of John was born 1737. However at Cornwood **William Philips** was baptized 17 Dec 1769 to John and Jane Philips. These men could be a possible father and grandfather. A James was baptized Nov 30 1768 to William and Thomasina Philips. There were no earlier records of Philips at Cornwood. However throughout the 1780's and 90's there were baptisms by William and Jenny; William and Elizabeth Bowden; William and Jane; Robert and Mary. All of the Philips were stone masons. So while there is nothing definitive, there are possible connections to Plymouth and Cornwood. Yet the most likely association would be the Philips family named at Peter Tavy because it was easy to get to Dury from there and they shared a lot of given names.

Then who are the parents and grandparents? A **hypothetical possibility # one** is that in 1751 Richard Philips married Sarah Chubb of Peter Tavy and they had a son William Philips in 1764 who as part of the couple, William and Anne Philips of Cornwood, 30 plus years later was father of William who lived at Dury farm in Lydford parish **or**

Hypothetical possibility # two is that it was Richard born 1767 who in 1841 lived as widower with his son Roger.

So as we can not go further back with evidence about William's family, let's move on to what we know about where he lived.

William Philips and his wife Elizabeth Waldron (or Waldon) were married January 11, 1829 at North Bovey Devon and known to be living at Dury farm in 1830. He was the tenant of the Duke of Cornwall. He and Elizabeth took their second child William to the church at Widecombe to be baptized on 28 November 1830. William Philips, Yeoman of Dury, Lydford was the father. Two years earlier his older child Richard had been baptized at Lydford on 22 March 1829 (he was born Feb 20 1829) and William Philips was classed as a laborer. So possibly this man of about 30 years of age and a free man had the money to rent Dury farm from the royal family about 1830. Mary the 3rd child was also baptized at Lydford on February 17, 1833 by William, Yeoman and Elizabeth. George was baptized 18 February 1835 at Lydford. John Philp was baptized Dec 24 1837 at Widecombe by William and Elizabeth. Other children's baptisms are not known. The other children possibly were baptized there as well but there is no found record. Perhaps they were never baptized although that would have been a concerning religious error.

It is possible Elizabeth Waldron had a brother John Waldron married to Mary and they lived at Cherry Brook house, Lydford parish with children John born 1825 and Henry 1829.

1841 census records stated their ages as **William Philips** 40 estimated, Elizabeth 35, Richard 12 (1829), William 10 (1830), Mary 8 (1833), George 6 (1835), John 3 (1838), James 1 (1840) plus John Thorn 15 and Mary Jenkins 20, a servant lad and lass. Make note of this because in later years these people had a problem in providing their birth year.

So who was yeoman Philips? A yeoman was a free tenant, usually a prominent farmer. As he worked with his hands, he could not be styled a gentleman but his status was above that of most other copyhold tenants. He was qualified to serve on juries and vote in county elections. While he did not outright own his land, his lease really allowed him to treat it as his own. To be able to lease his own farm outright meant he had the financial backing to do it. He was no share cropper renting land.

Dury was not just any farm. It was one of the surviving Ancient Tenements, the oldest surviving farms in Dartmoor. There were 34 of them established in the 14th century and possibly earlier, a few remain.

In Mediaeval Britain, grazing rights within the boundaries of the Forest of Dartmoor were strictly limited. However a few settlers were permitted to build farms there and to release their livestock on surrounding land. These farms became known as the Ancient Tenements. Today some of the ancient tenements are still a working farm: Babeny, Pizwell, Huccaby, Dunnabridge, Brimpts, Runnage, Merripit, Sherberton and Dury. Other such as Brownberry and Warner have long gone and Hexworthy has now grown into a village.

For centuries these settlements were isolated from 'civilization' - many miles from the nearest villages. And yet the inhabitants were still expected to travel many miles over hills and rough terrain to attend church each Sunday. The Forest of Dartmoor no longer was regarded as a Royal Forest but became a chase. Confusingly, the term 'Forest' was and is still used to describe the chase which was divided up initially into 3 quarters (later 4). In 1240 the bounds of the 'Forest' were set out and a perambulation of its limits were carried out. At about this time the first of the Ancient Tenements was established which also coincided with the increased pressure on food supplies. John Somers Cocks considered that there are two pieces of evidence for this date. Firstly there is the document of 1260 which was a petition to Bishop Bronsecombe of Exeter. This petition came from the inhabitants of two of the earlier tenements of Pizwell and Babeny and it asked permission to use the nearer church of Widecombe as opposed to Lydford. The Bishop consented to this request and official dispensation was given in a document called 'The Ordinacio de Lydford' which was dated the 20th of August 1260. Therefore if this document records the ancient tenements of Pizwell and Babeny, they must have been in existence by that date which can be considered as firm dating evidence. Somers Cocks' second piece of dating evidence is more tenuous insomuch as he states: 'Of the many sites of Farms founded from about the 11th century and abandoned by about 1300, none has been discovered within the Forest, though the territory would seem perfectly suitable. Clearly some policy must have up until then prevented what surely otherwise have been attempted.' From the period between 1260 and 1563 there were 17 tenement groups established but then within these were several individual farmsteads which brings the total to 34 or 35.

Dury was recorded for the first time in 1390 under the notation "teram de Dury". Later the terms were spelled out:

"On these tenements there are several ancient houses, on each of which said thirty five tenements several parcels of waste ground, enclosed chiefly with stone walls many hundred years since, as it appears by ancient deeds and writings related to the same, according to the ancient use and custom of the Forest. The heir of each and every of the said tenants, on the death of each of the said tenants, and every purchaser that shall purchase the inheritance of any such ancient tenements, have by the custom aforesaid liberty to enclose eight acres of the said waste or forest ground…. paying one shilling yearly fro the same to her Majesty's use… which said eight is commonly called the newtake… The enclosing of such newtake doth generally cost such taker £20, and doth not yield above 20s, per annum when enclosed… The tenants collect and gather the rent, and pay it at Exeter. They attend the three weeks court at the Castle of Lydford. They must assist in the drives of the east, south and west quarters four days in the year, each finding a man, horse, and servant at their own costs, save only a halfpenny cake each forest man or driver hath according to the said custom. They likewise drive all the colts, one day in the year to one of her Majesty's pounds, and some are driven as much as twenty miles. They attend three times a year at Lydford Castle Court to present all matters and misdemeanours and things presentable in the Forest. They present all estrays at the next law court… By ancient and long accustomed law and usage of the said Forest, there are only three sorts of people that have a right to depasture their cattle on the said Forest of Dartmoor; that is to say, forestmen, to wit, the occupiers of the said thirty five tenements, their predecessors and successors, who are at present

Queen's immediate tenants..."

Did William acquire the right to be the tenant from his father? Was William in 1831 considered a Forest Man, a tenant who gained his right to the farm from his father. It would be necessary to see the records of the Duchy of Cornwall to find this out.

So what type of farming was going on in the early days of the ancient tenements?

"We know that there was a buoyant livestock industry on Dartmoor from a document of 1340 which states that the forty four tenants depastured 4,700 oxen and 37 steers on Dartmoor, (Burnard, p. 35). But it is suggested that the fields of the tenements were, 'as islands in the sea' because these enclosures were surrounded by cornditches which separated them from the 'sea of rough pasture', upon which the livestock grazed, (Fox, 1994, p.154). But how do we know that the farmers were growing crops in these fields? Once again Fox notes that there is documentary evidence in the form of an account dating from 1304 which records a mill that was newly constructed at Babeny. It also states that the mill was built at the tenants expense apart from the timber which came from the King's wood and that in order to remain autonomous from manorial extortion paid 33s 4d annually for the privilege. It is plain to see that if there must have been a significant degree of arable farming taking place for such an expense to be met. Further evidence for the mill exists in the modern landscape as many of its features are still visible."

William raised his family at Dury farm. He lived there for at least 20 years. His children were raised there and he was recorded as having young people working for him as well. The census records a farm boy helper and a young house or dairy maid living with the family. That was considered normal in the mid 1800's.

William's house was ancient. It was described as having an ancient fireplace and a flight of granite stairs winding around the chimney stack. These were medieval features. Many of the tenement farms were described as of lowly construction with granite walls and thatch roof. Often the home and the barn were attached as one living area. Since there were no roads, there were no wheeled vehicles. A wood plow was used and horses or oxen were used to pull sledges. It would take up to ten oxen to pull the plow. A flail was used to harvest grain by hand. Dung pots carried the manure from the residence/barn by a shoulder yoke to be emptied on the fields. Cattle and sheep were the principle animals and income was supplemented by collecting lichens from the rocks to be sold for making dye and moss was gathered for stuffing mattresses. Peat was cut and burned in the hearth. People with stone skills gathered and cut granite rocks to sell. In general the cluster of Ancient Tenements around Post Bridge were on fairly good agricultural land and so made a decent living but in general this was a poor area for farming and between 1830 and 1855 more than 10 000 people emigrated from North Devon to Canada.

Since William's father may have been a stone mason, William possibly was also. These people shaped the stones for building as opposed to a quarry man who excavated the rocks from the mine.

Other Philips family details are also recorded. The father of a John Philips was said to have found a deposit of China clay which he mined commencing in 1834. John Philips began to make sanitary ware (white pottery) from this clay. He may have lived at Peter Tavy, a hamlet on the edge of the moor. Later at the turn of the 20th century a William Phillips took charge of the Dartmoor Hunt as Master of the Hunt and Tom Phillips was also involved with the hunt. What connection these had with our William is not known.

About the time William and his family left for Canada an existing unused prison was reactivated to house convicts. This prison provided work for people on the moor. So for William and his family there seemed to be no great reason to relocate.

Why did William Philips, a man in his 50's with semi-grown children, decide to leave Devon? He appeared to have a fairly decent farm and livelihood.

The answer may lie in an event that happened in 1844. At that time the Duke of Cornwall convinced the British parliament to allow him to sell some property and renegotiate some of his leases to tenants. At some point Dury farm became privately owned as it can be sold freely today. My thought is Dury farm may have been put on the market and the lease terminated by the Duke. William, while able to make a living, was not able to purchase the farm outright and so had to give up his lease. The settlement to terminate the lease, which may be recorded someplace, possibly included enough for a passage fare for the entire family to go settle in Canada. Or the lease may have naturally lapsed and he used his life savings to pay for his passage. Or like many he was subsidized to vacate England with cheap steerage accommodations.

So before we move on, what sort of place is Dury farm today? In the 21st

Century it was described this way:

"Dury Farm, near Postbridge, in the very heart of the Moor, is home to Shelagh and Martyn Longly, who would be the first to agree that they feel privileged to live in this unique location, but that it is not for the faint-hearted! The farm consists of 46 hectares of upland, organic land, lying between 1000 and 1200 feet and bisected by the East Dart river. There are 30 ha of improved land (of which 20 ha are accessible for cutting) and 16 ha of rough grazing. The whole farm is in an UOELS scheme with 13 ha of river valley managed under an HLS agreement. The average rainfall is 75-85 inches."

Then in 2019 it went on the market:

Situation
Dury Farm is situated in the heart of Dartmoor National Park in a truly wonderful moorland setting. The village of Postbridge has a shop / post office, a public house, church, village hall and a National Park Visitors' Information Centre. Being situated in the heart of Dartmoor National Park, there are many thousands of beautiful, unspoilt moorland acres on the doorstep in which to enjoy a wide range of outdoor pursuits including walking, riding, cycling and fishing.

The town of Moretonhampstead has a good range of dayto day amenities including restaurants, a swimming pool, sports centre, health centre, primary school and dental,doctors and veterinary practices. Other nearby towns and villages include Princetown, Chagford, Widecombe in the Moor and Tavistock.

Introduction
Dury Farm lies in a beautiful and secluded location surrounded by open moor. It is one of the few freehold farms and one of five ancient tenements on the moor. It was first mentioned in documents in 1344. In Reg Bellamy's book 'Postbridge The Heart of Dartmoor' the farm house is recorded as being probably on the site of an old longhouse, that fell into disrepair in the early 1900s and was eventually restored by Stones of Chagford (builders).
The current owners have made many improvements to the properties during their 13 year tenure, including complete modernization of the farmhouse, including the addition of a bio-mass heating system, creating a spacious and comfortable family home. There is slate flooring throughout the ground floor with underfloor heating.

Brook Cottage has been completely renovated and offers excellent secondary accommodation with the potential for holiday use.

The land extends to approximately 114.5 acres and provides excellent grassland and as well as amenity land close to the East Dart River offering conservation appeal.

The Farmhouse
The property is accessed via a covered porch leading to the Entrance Hall with door through to the Kitchen with a bespoke hand-made set of floor units with slate worktop incorporating a Miele integrated dishwasher, Liebherr integrated fridge and Britannia Range electric oven with 6-burner LPG gas hob. Large archway through to Dining Room which is a very light room with views over the terraced lawn area with oak and glazed doors into the sitting room. Utility Room with sink and space for fridge/freezer. Space and plumbing for washing machine and tumble dryer. Door to cloakroom. The super Sitting Room has patio doors leading to the rear decked area and to a sheltered deck for enjoying the afternoon and evening sun. Further archway leads through to the Snug with slate fireplace and oak over mantle and working wood-burning stove. Windows
overlooking the front garden and recessed built in cupboards. Door to Study with fireplace and the potential for a wood-burning stove to be installed. This room could be knocked through (subject to any necessary consents) to the adjoining store room to create a granny annexe, as the electric and water points have been brought into the store room. Main Hallway with stairs rising to first floor with under stairs cupboard housing all the underfloor heating controls. The oak staircase rises to the first floor landing which is laid with solid oak flooring and continues through all the first floor bedrooms. Master Bedroom with windows to two sides, ample space for free standing furniture and door to en-suite Bathroom with separate corner shower and Velux windows. Door to Bedroom 2 with windows overlooking the front garden. Bedroom 4 currently laid out as a twin room with two Velux windows. Connecting door on the landing providing access to Bedroom 3, large storage cupboard and Family Bathroom with separate corner shower.

Outbuildings
To the side of Dury Farm there is a double car port with ample space for two large vehicles with wood storage to the rear and door to boiler room which houses the ETA bio-mass boiler and AKVA 3000 heat store, which provides heating and hot water for the house and cottage.

Gardens and Grounds
To the rear of the car port are some raised herb/vegetable beds and a decked
pathway which extends all the way to the sheltered larger decked area which
is accessed from the sitting room. This area has a damp proof course and
footings already in place should the successful purchaser
wish to convert this covered area to a garden room or conservatory, for
example. Fantastic views are enjoyed over the terraced lawned area with an
abundance of granite stone walling being a particular feature of the
property. The gardens surround the property on all sides, offering much
sought after protection and seclusion. Bounded by granite stone walls. There
is a recently planted area of broad leafed trees and a Beech hedge, screening
off Brook Cottage from the property.

"Dury Farm at Postbridge is a Dartmoor gem in the heart of the park. This great property included a modernised traditional farmhouse, recently refurbished cottage, and range of buildings set in 114 acres of excellent grassland running down to the East Dart River. It sold off a guide price of £1.3 million."

Dury Farm as it was in 2020.

The modern Dury is a far different farm than when William and his family left it.

In 1851 William and Elizabeth appear in the census as a broken family unit. William Philp says he was born in Tavistock, age 53 in 1798. He farms 50 acres at Dury and likely could pasture on more land. Elizabeth is 50 and was born in Lidford. At home are Richard 22 ,William 20, Mary 19, John 12, James 10, and Grace 8.

George age 16 has left home and found work with Robert Perkin of Tavistock who farms 400 acres and has six young children as well as 10 servants and farm workers. George is employed as a farm servant, a boy who would help out around the farm for a year or two.

William and Elizabeth have a family where the older children need work and the younger are fast growing up. Apparently their future is not to be at Dury farm or in Devon but across the sea in Canada.

When they left for Canada, there were other Phillips living around Lydford parish. Roger and John remained raising families and could have been close relatives.

Since the Napoleonic war and by 1850, 800 000 people had left England for Canada. More than 10 000 had left north Devon. William and Elizabeth were not alone in leaving. Much of the good farm land in eastern Canada had already been settled.

Why the entire family packed up and left is not known. There were essentially two ways to travel to Canada. One way was subsidized passage as poor people traveling as steerage or another way was pay your own way which was about 7 pounds each or in 2020 equal to 945 pounds. The fare for a family of this size would amount to about $10-12 000 dollars today which in 1852 was a considerable sum. The typical farm wages were more like10 shillings a month so the fare was equal to about 1 years wages.

Departures for Canada could be arranged from Plymouth or Bideford on the north Devon coast which was farther to travel but there was a shipping company there that specialized in passengers to Quebec one way and then returned with lumber the other. Several trips were made each summer. We don't know if they traveled from either of these ports.

The North Devon exodus began in 1830. Thomas Burnard Chanter advertised in the North Devon Journal that his ships Collina, Calypso, Sappho and Euphemia had been "conveniently fitted up for Families and will take out passengers on moderate terms". This was because the ships were used to import timber from Canada and had no cargo to go the other way. The Bideford ships made the round trip about two or three times during the summer season which began when the ice in the Gulf of St. Lawrence broke up.

One possibility is the barque Secret which sailed on April 3rd and arrived at Quebec City on May 5th. An account of the departure of the Secret appeared in the North Devon Journal of April 8, 1852:

"DEPARTURE OF THE 'SECRET.'—At five o'clock on Saturday morning, amidst the firing of cannon, and cheering of those on board the emigrant ship, the 'Secret,' was towed as far as the pool by the 'Princess Royal,' and in the afternoon of the same day the voyagers to Yankeeland has the honour of being joined by a little stranger who had just come into the world to make the voyage of life by commencing it on the seas, to be rocked and cradled by its waves, whilst the wild winds sing its lullaby. We refer to the fact of a Mrs. Wilton giving birth to a fine son, who, in honor of the event, was named John Secret Wilton. On Monday, she crossed the bar and crowded all sail for her destination. The afternoon being beautifully fine, several of our townsmen accompanied her to a distance of four of five miles. At last the time came for parting; and, after a few interchanges of cheering sentiments, and the sincerest expressions of goodwill, they parted company, those on board the 'Secret' firing a salute as a last farewell. We also say 'farewell;' and, whilst they think of their friends at home and anticipate the land of their hopes, we will sing—

God speed ye, brethren, o'er the main;
We never more may meet again,
But, if kind prayers avail,
This morning orisons shall rise,
And piece the circumanbient skies,—
God send a prosperous gale!

We are happy to find that so many   have already started under such auspicious circumstances, and that it is our province to say "Still there is room." The 'Worthy' has a few berths to spare. A word to the wise in enough; and, therefore, to those intending to emigrate this season we have no need to say—Take time by the forelock!"

Another possibility is the Worthy of Devon which departed Bideford on April 17th and arrived at Quebec in early June. On its second voyage of the year the Worthy arrived at Quebec City on July 22nd after a passage of 26 days. Both were owned by Richard Heard of Bideford, a timber merchant.

The Secret made a second voyage to Quebec that year, departing Bideford on July 11th.

Advertisements frequently appeared in the North Devon Journal promising: *...excellence of the accommodations, the approved sailing qualities of their vessels, the ability and civility of their commanders, and the exceedingly low rate of passage required, are advantages which persons about to cross the Atlantic from these parts will be likely to appreciate.*

On the return voyage the ships carried pine, oak and birch logs that Heard would then sell in his Bideford timber yard.

There is no evidence that the Phillips family went that way. They may well have shipped out from Plymouth or some other port. However their

-18-

circumstances may well fit the description given above and it is believed that they sailed in 1852. The chances of it being a sailing ship were greater than going by steam.

In 1852 it was possible to acquire land in the Huron Tract almost free. This was virgin land that needed clearing and homesteading but the Phillips family did not undertake that effort. The Canada Company that arranged passage and tools and assistance to take up the land in the Huron Tract ought to have been known to William but they did not pursue that option. So some other factor was at work.

Why did they travel to Ingersoll and Oxford County to make their new home? What was so special about this location? My assumption was they knew people who had come before.

They arrived in Ingersoll quite possibly on one of the first trains in town on the newly completed Grand Trunk Western railroad. They had just completed a journey of some weeks to come thousands of miles to Oxford county Ontario. Were they met by anyone? We are not even certain of the year 1852 or 3 or slightly later. Why south of Ingersoll?

Again this is an unknown, but a Richard Phillips had been enumerated in 1861 about lot 17 Concession 1 of Dereham Twp. on property near Hagles corner they did not own. He was 70 and his wife Ann 68. With them were adult children ranging in age from 40 down to 20. None were married but they had named these children in almost the same order as William and Elizabeth had done with theirs: Richard, William, Mary, George, John, Joseph (vs James), Catherine, Grace the last child. This is a very odd coincidence. Moreover this family had not been long in Ontario from England as they were not in the 1851 census. They also could not be found in the England census of 1841 or 51. Their son Richard later bought a farm near the center of Dereham Township. Tanners from Devon and connected to Lydford also were living in the West Oxford and Dereham area.

Now recall that earlier in the story I mentioned the 1841 census where Richard was living with his son Roger not far from Dury whose children were named: Richard, Mary, William, James, John and Thomas. Another odd naming coincidence or was it some sort of family pattern.

William was reported to have settled at Peebles, a place name, where west Oxford Township met Dereham Twp. at Folden road. This was pointed out to me anecdotally by Donald Phillips a descendant. Research has shown that

William's oldest son Richard lived at that location. This was the same neighborhood as Richard age 70 had lived, perhaps same road. Did they all come together? Were they even related? Was Richard senior, Williams older brother?

It is assumed they arrived in 1852. The evidence for that was reported in the census of 1901 by William Phillips Jr. but others thought 1853 or 1856.

Richard, William and Elizabeth's oldest child, married Susan Tanner presumably at Foldens as Wesleyan Methodists. The groom was Richard Phillips 28 of West Oxford son of William Phillips and Elizabeth Waldon (This is the only evidence of her maiden name as Waldon). The bride was Susan Tanner 22 of Ingersoll, born in Devonshire and daughter of George Tanner and Elizabeth Davis. The witnesses were Martin Tanner and Mary Ann Tanner of Dereham, presumably the bride's brother and wife. The Rev. George Kennedy was the minister. This took place on October 14, 1858.

There were other Tanner- Phillips marriages so here is more background on Tanners. Mary Ann Tanner, Martin's wife, had been born in Lydford to Zacharia and Mary Pascoe in 1828. They also came to Canada. More than one Lydford family had come to Oxford. Martin was born May 10 1826 in Lidford and came to Canada 1856-8 with his sister Susan and brother George and farmed in North Dorchester in 1870 and 80s. The family was buried at West Oxford United Church Cemetery, Centerville. In 1861 Martin and Mary Ann were living in Ingersoll east of downtown, south of the river but farming elsewhere. Daughters Mary Anne 9, Louisa 6, Eliza 4 were born in England and John 2 was born in Canada. Next door were George Tanner 27 (27 May 1832) and his wife Mary Ann 21 who was born in Canada as well as Elizabeth 5 and George 3 indicating an arrival in Canada by 1856. Other younger children were Susan Jane, Sarah, Martha, James and another George. The Tanner parents father George died 1848 in England and their mother Elizabeth Davis Tanner came to Canada with the children.

George Tanner born 1796 and Elizabeth Davis also 1796 were married at Widecombe in the Moor 27 Nov 1815. Their children were mostly born at Lydford, specifically in 1823 twin girls Elizabeth and Marianne were born at Princetown which was in Dartmoor near Dury and then Martin 1824, and John 1826. Most of the other children, Louise or Lewisa 1829, George 1832 and Susan or Susannah 1835 were at home in 1841 living at Ring Hill farm near Princetown. Ring Hill Farm was just north of the Philips at Dury at Postbridge. So the emigration was the effort of two neighbors. The Tanner family came about 1856-7.

One person who did not come was George Tanner, the father of Susan George and Martin. He had died by 1851 when son George was at home with his mother and sisters. Young George was working as a tin miner an occupation that as an 18 year old he did not likely care for. So when the opportunity to go to Canada came, he was anxious to go with his older brother Martin and sister Susan. We now go back to the Phillips family.

After arriving in Ontario William Phillips and Elizabeth Waldron's family, nearly all adults, soon began to disperse and marry. By the 1861 census the children had moved on and some had settled down. William and Elizabeth were not found in the 1861 census but it was thought they lived south of Ingersoll or in that village. The children were now mostly in their 20's. Mary 33 and Grace 18 from Dereham Township were lodgers in West Oxford with Joel Wright who also boarded John Wells a school teacher. It would be normal for the girls to be living with their parents but they are not. Although most homes were still log cabins, the Phillips were living in frame homes. Next door to Mary and Grace in 1861 were their brother Richard and wife Susan and two young boys. The problem a few years after arriving was the whereabouts of the parents William and Elizabeth.

Later in that year 1861 on Nov 25 Mary, reported as born in 1835 (actually 1833), wed John Richardson 29,(1832) whose parents were Peter Richardson and Elizabeth Foster of Yorkshire. However the census of 1861 showed a John Richardson 28 laborer from England working for William Wilkerson in West Oxford. His parents could not be found in the census of the spring of 1861 in Oxford county. Mary's mother was noted as Elizabeth Waldron but elsewhere she was Waldon. Later in this story it will be seen that a John Richardson mortgaged/sold lot 6 con 1 Dereham to Mary's brother Richard. The location where Richard Phillips seemingly had been living for some time.

So where were the parents, William and Elizabeth in 1861? There is no record found in the census and they do not appear to be recorded any where yet they both died in Ontario.

Life on the farm in the 1860's, 70's and 80's was a life of self sufficiency. Earned money came from the sale of the excess from the farm of which there was not very much. In the census of 1871 a typical 100 or so acre farm was about all a couple could manage and still raise their large families. Here is a typical production output from a south western Ontario farm taken from the 1861 census data.

"On the farm there was listed one house, built in 1861, two barns, one carriage, two wagons, a plough, two mowers or reapers, a horse rake and a fanning mill. 45 acres were under the plough, 20 were pasture, 9 acres were in wheat, 30 in barley, 8 in peas and there was an orchard. 50 bu. of corn and 70 bu. of potatoes were grown on half an acre. 10 acres of hay produced 20 tons. 100 lbs of grapes were grown which produced 5 gal of wine. 150 lbs of maple syrup were produced. The farmer owned that year 2 adult horses, 3 milk cows, 8 horned cattle, 12 sheep, and some pigs. The farmer sold 6 cattle, 2 sheep, and five pigs. The farm produced 300 lbs of butter. 20 lbs of wool were produced and turned into 20 yards of cloth by the farmer's wife. 35 cords of firewood were cut."

This was the record of a self sufficient family surviving on their own effort. While not pioneers, they were not far removed from those days. Many still lived in log cabins but frame and some brick homes were replacing them.

William Phillips Sr. died in 1864 September 28. The cemetery known as the Ingersoll Rural Cemetery had just opened in August but he was not the first burial. Elizabeth survived for some time. She went to live with one of her children, Grace Atkinson, who lived in Middlesex county. Elizabeth died there but was buried in the Ingersoll Rural Cemetery which contains the graves of a number of Phillips relatives particularly those who went to the Methodist Church at Folden's Corner. Elizabeth died Nov 20, 1883.

In looking at the census for 1861 it was clear the family had set off to each make their own way in Ontario.

So what became of the children of William and Elizabeth Philips. You will discover that they used both Philips, and Phillips, and possibly Philps for spelling and sometimes they dropped the s. The last one could also be Phelps.

What became of Mary Philips?

It had been thought that Mary died in 1878 in Ingersoll but the Mary who died in Ingersoll April 29th 1878 age 43, was Mary E. Richardson 4 years 3 months old. Her father John Richardson lived until 1906 dying in East Zorra and he was buried in Ingersoll Rural He was married to Ann Bailey who was Irish and was living with him in East Zorra in 1871. (not on the 1876 map for East or West Zorra). It took some effort to discover but it seems Mary Phillips who married John Richardson actually lived near St. George, Brant county after her marriage and died there much later. While they were married in late 1861, there were no children until later. It can not be conclusively proven this is the correct Mary Phillips but there is no other John and Mary in the counties adjacent that fit the description and no other Phillips-Richardson Ontario marriage recorded in the 1860's.

Ontario records that a John Richardson and a Mary Philips gave birth to Elizabeth Ann Richardson April 22 1870 and a Peter Thomas Richardson, May 25 1873. Both children were born in South Dumfries, Brant County to the dairyman/farmer.

In the 1871 census of South Dumfries Brant Co. it is reported that John Richardson was 38 (b. 1833) Mary Richardson 34 (b.1837) and both were born in England. Their children were Peter 5 (1866), William 3(1868), Ann newborn (1871). Plus there was one James Philips, her brother?, age 26 (b.1845) living with them; however, there also was a James Philips age 28 living with the Atkinson's near Embro in 1871. Could he have been counted twice? The census took place over a period of time in April. Or are they two different people?

Ten years later 1881 after Mary was thought dead, (see above) their family had changed. There was no Peter age 15. William was 14, Robert 10 ,Annie Philip12 and now there was a Peter 7. It was not unusual to name the next child after the one who died. Also depending on the birth month it was common for a census birth record to be out a year. Census' were taken in the spring.

In 1891 at home in South Dumfries were John 59, Mary 56 and Peter 17. No others were there.

It was reported that on May 26th 1896 John Richardson, cheese maker South Dumfries, died of nephritis. His wife Mary Phillips Richardson died Dec 2 1897 and they are buried in St. George's Cemetery, St George, Ontario.

So by going back and cross referencing census, burials, and births, and discarding several other possibilities, Mary likely did not die in 1878 and the John Richardson in the Ingersoll Rural was not her husband. Mary married a different John Richardson also in Oxford county. They settled near St. George, actually the first farm west of the village (now an industrial subdivision) where her farmer husband was also a cheese maker and her brother James went there for a time before moving to Middlesex county by 1881 to also become a cheese maker.

None of this may prove correct but the accumulated evidence appears to make the above a strong case based on the facts.

Notes

Where was William Phillips Jr.?

William Philips was not found in the 1861 census but his marriage to Frances Burtch of Dereham took place 4th March of 1863. Her age was reported as 19 (later she said born 1841). He was reported as born 1837 (actual was 1831) and was age 26. Her parents were Benjamin and Anna Burtch who had family in the Folden's area where William's brother and sister had been living. This was a double wedding as Grace Phillips his sister, age 18 (actual 20) married Francis Atkinson of Dereham Twp. Both weddings were by John Edwards of the Bible Christian church on March 4th 1863.

After the marriage of Frances and William, he found work as a farmer near Crumlin and in 1871 was living on the north side of Highway 2 just east of the Crumlin road east of London, Ontario. Here he remained for some time. In 1871 his family consisted of William 39, Frances now age 29 who was born in Ireland and they were listed as Baptists. The children were Sarah Anne 9, Francis Edwin 7, William Benjamin 5, Charles Herbert 3, Albert Henry, 5 months born the previous November. Living with them was his wife's sister Rebecca Burtch 26. They lived in a house, lot 9 con 6 London Township on the land of either W. Stevenson or Henry Burgess and presumably worked or rented from one of them. How he came to find farm work there is not known. A decade on his family had grown and his neighbors were now the Shoebottoms and Edward Roberts. William was 44 having only aged 5 years, Frances was 39, Sarah Anne 18, Francis 17, Wm. Benjamin 15, Charles 12, Albert 10, and Walter James 5 and John 3 months having been born in January 1881. In the 1891 census either they had moved a little east or their neighbors had changed to Guest and Talbot. Wm. Phillips was now 60, Frances 49, and living at home were Benjamin 25, Sarah 28, Charles 22, Albert 20, Walter 15, Mable 5. All but Mable were literate and they were now listed as Church of England. Francis was no longer at home and children were listed with their preferred name use.

The 1901 census provides some new details. William says he was born 15 Nov. 1831. However earlier records show he was baptized 28 Nov 1830. He also reported arriving in Canada in 1852. He and Frances were Anglican and still farming at age 70 and 59. Frances was born in Ontario 12 Aug. 1841. At home still were Charles born 20 May 1868 age 32 listed as Methodist. Albert 29 Nov. 1870 age 30 was a Baptist. Walter J. 21 June 1874 was age 25 attending Church of England. Mabel was born 3 Sept. 1885 was 15 and a

Methodist. Interesting that there were 3 different religions in the household. Their neighbors were James Shoebottom and Samuel Stanley.

In 1905 their son Walter James Phillips 29 married Sarah Shoebottom 25 daughter of John and Rebecca Shoebottom. The next generation was forming.

Frances died Nov 7 1915 and William Feb 27, 1918 age 86. They are buried at St. John's Cemetery Arva Ontario.

If you are interested in what became of any of their children who have been documented above try searching the census reports of Canada 1911, and 1921.

Notes

Where was Grace Phillips Atkinson?

Grace as mentioned was married in a double wedding with her brother William. She married Francis Atkinson age 23(1840) son of Christopher and Frances Atkinson from Cumberland, England on March 4th 1863 but living in the Dereham / West Oxford area. The Atkinson's began their married life in the Embro area. Christopher was born 1864, then James 1866, and Henry 1869 who when he was married in 1899 lived in Toronto where he was a salesman and said he had been born at Embro.

In the census of 1871 the Atkinsons were living in West Zorra and the family included Francis 36, Grace 27, Christopher 7, James 5, Henry 4, Frances 2, and William born October 1870. Grace's mother Elizabeth Philips was also living with them as her William had died not long after Grace's wedding. Brother James Philips was also deemed to be living there as a 28 year old laborer. Also in their household was Robert Harris and his wife who were 19. Elizabeth was listed as Episcopalian but the rest of the family were Wesleyan Methodists. The area where they were living was heavily populated with emigrants from Scotland. They lived on the west side of the 6th Concession on either lot 10 or 11, just east of Embro and possibly rented from Capt. Gordon or Angus Campbell. Some time after 1871 and before 1878 they relocated to Caradoc Township. Both Francis Atkinson and James Philips relocated to Middlesex county. Francis's farm was on what is now known as Parkhouse drive at the corner of Melbourne road. This was 5 roads south and a couple of lots west of property James may have bought on Inadale Drive. They were there for the census of 1881.

The Atkinson household in 1881 consisted of Francis born 1832 in England age 49, Grace 35, Christopher 17, James 15, Henry 13, Francis 11, William 10, Elizabeth 9, Charles 7, Robert 5, and Mary A. 1. All were listed as Wesleyan Methodists. Also with them was Grace's mother Elizabeth Philips 80 and Francis Thompson 50.

Ten years on, there were changes to the family. Grace's mother Elizabeth had died Nov 20 1883 and they took her to Ingersoll to be buried with her husband. The Atkinson family could not be found in the 1881 census.

In 1899 son Henry, now a salesman in Toronto wed Elizabeth Langdon on June 12.

In 1901 the family was on Con 1 Ekfrid Township in the village of Melbourne. Frances reported his birthday was 14 Feb. 1834,owned his own farm, was a Methodist and born in England. Likewise Grace reported she was born 18 March 1840 (She was 8 in1851 census so 1843 would be more accurate). Still at home were Charles 26, 12 July 1872, Robert 24, 12 October 1876, George 19, 27 Feb 1882, Edgar J.15, 23 June 1885 and Fanny 22, 16 September 1878.

Grace died March 29 1904 after having been paralyzed for 2 years. Her age was given as 63. Francis lived until July 30 1917 when he died of pneumonia while he was living at the home of his son Robert of 570 Pall Mall St. London Ontario. He was buried in the Longwood Cemetery in Caradoc Twp.

Their son George Phillips born 1882 married Bertha ? and was a stationary engineer at an oil company in Sarnia where he died age 52 on June 17, 1935. William moved back to Oxford county and lived in West Oxford for 17 years , Lot 8 Con 3. He died Nov 4, 1924 having been in poor health for some time. Robert Atkinson moved to London and Charles moved to Eastwood (Woodstock)

If you are interested in what became of any of Grace's other children who have been documented above try searching the census reports of Canada 1911 and 1921.

Notes

Where was George Philps?

George went by the name Philps and was born in 1835. He claimed 1833. George made his way to Woodstock where on Nov. 13, 1861 he married Ellen Hamlin, born 1841, daughter of Elias and Susan Hamlin. George at his marriage was living in Ingersoll. In 1871 Ellen and George Philps were living in East Zorra Twp. north of County rd 33 on the east west Zorra line about lot 12 Con 9. This was just east of his sister. George said he was 35 a Methodist, Ellen was 31. Their children were James 11, Walter 8, Thomas 6, Albert 4. This farm was likely rented. They may have previously lived in Ingersoll as Albert was born there.

Like his relatives he too headed off to Middlesex county and was there in 1881, this time in Ekfrid Twp. also near Melbourne, the location not certain. One reason for all these relocations was the fact that there was still original farmland to be had from the Canada Company although some was second owner purchasers. There were no more children but Elizabeth Park age 6 was living with them. A Tanner family had also relocated to Ekfrid. The connection is not known. James went to live in Strathroy. Walter never married and became a horse dealer. He was taking his buggy beside the GTR tracks at the townline of Ekfrid and Caradoc and unaware of the coming train turned to cross the tracks. Hit directly he was thrown a hundred feet and died Feb. 4 1907. Thomas became a minister and went to the west. He married Alecia Emmaline Richards 1872 - 1970. Their son Winston Richards Philps died age 18 in 1926 (b. 1907).Their youngest Albert lived on the home farm a mile and a half north of Melbourne.

There is a tomb in the Longwoods Cemetery indicating George Philps died 9 Jan 1886 age 53.With it is a tomb for Ellen Philps died 16 Dec 1900. Ellen could not be found in the 1891 census.

Albert Philps, their youngest child, was married 28 May 1897 at Longwood. He said he was 28, born Sept 15 1868 in Ingersoll. Albert was a farmer in Adelaide Twp. and his wife Mary Warren 27 was the daughter of Henry Warren and Mary Hirshman of Adelaide Twp. Middlesex Co. In April 1901 Albert was the father of newborn Rose at lot 2 Con 2 Caradoc, essentially next door to the Atkinson farm.

Albert is buried in the Longwoods cemetery and died 31 January 1952. Mary Warren Philps died 3 Sept 1951. Their children: Rose 1900-1973 married George Seburn 1883 - 1953, Gladys married George Olde, George Philps and Warren Philps 1913 died 17 Nov 1982 married Alice Eliza Kellerstein 1917-2005.

The next generation is recorded in the descendants section.

Notes

Where was John Phillips?

John was born in 1838 although he later seems to think he was born in 1842. A John Philips 19 was working for the Poole family at Hagles Corners in1861 and during the year it appears the senior Pool had died. John married Tabitha Taylor of Ingersoll Dec 24,1868. She was daughter of Mark and Tabitha Taylor. He stated he was 25 and thus born 1843. She was 21. They were farming in Dereham Township in 1871 where son Charles was born in 1869-70. They moved to South Dorchester Twp. by 1881 where William Gordon Philips was born on April 5 1881. John was likely a tenant farmer. By 1883 he homesteaded to Fuller Twp., Codington Co. South Dakota. This was new territory being settled by people mostly from the eastern USA and Canada. In 1900 it was reported that he was 64 and was born in June of 1836, had come from Canada and was a farmer. Tabitha reported she had birthed 9 children of whom 4 were living. She reported her birth as November 1846 in Canada. They owned their farm free and clear. Living with them was their son Frederick age 21 born September 1878 in Canada. In 1900 he was not living with his parents. He died in 1940. A daughter Nettie May only lived 3 years 1879 to 1882. There were apparently other deceased children.

Also with them in 1900 was daughter Lois M. who had been born Sept. 1874 in Canada. She was the mother of 2 boys Jessie Minor Sept. 1894 and William Minor, October 1895. Their father William Jesse Minor was born in Wisconsin but died in 1896. Lois, 1874-1930, was reported as a widow in 1900 and later married Albert Christian and she became Lois Amelia Phillips Christian. Consequently she owned the Minor farm next to her father. Another of Tabitha's children was Earl DeWayne Phillips who was born August 1892 in SD and died in 1962. Tabitha would have been 46 when he was born. Earl was thus a playmate of his nephews as a child.

John's farm and his daughter's land were in section 18 near Lake Nicholson SD and between it and Dry Lake next to Phipps township. The Phillips home at 162nd street is gone but the Minor farm buildings are on 443 Ave. John died July 15, 1909 and is buried in the Lake Nicholson Cemetery with Tabitha who died 9 Sept. 1914. Other family members are buried there.

John and Tabitha Phillips

More grave information for John's family is at:
https://www.findagrave.com/memorial/64179184/john-phillips

Any of his children in the USA could be traced by US census. If you are interested in what became of any of their children in Canada, try searching the census reports of Canada 1911 and 1921.

Notes

Where was James Philips?

James was born 1840 or early1841 as he was in the census of 1841. James reported in 1901 he did not know his birthday. In 1871 he is possibly reported twice reported ages 26 (1845) and 28 (1847) He married Elizabeth Ann Tanner of Ingersoll born, July 22, 1856. He died 1924 in Middlesex County and his grave said he was born 1844. His farm was thought to be the second farm east of Melbourne road on Inadale Drive. It is a property that he may have bought from the Canada Land Company. It appears James learned to be a cheese maker, perhaps from his brother- in- law John Richardson of St. George with whom James lived as a young man. In the 1881 census he was living on Inadale Dr just south of Mayfair Rd in Metcalfe Twp. Here he was working as a cheese maker. He was living but a few kilometers from his sister and mother at the Atkinson farm. Where was he in 1871? Possibly he was living in Brant with John Richardson but a James, also a cheese maker, was living with the Atkinsons at Embro in 1871. This conflict may be a double census recording of him or there is an issue with the Richardson connection. Two years later 1873 he married Elizabeth Tanner age 27. He said was 38 and that his parents were William and Elizabeth Phillips and that they were born in England. Elizabeth Tanner was from in Ingersoll ON but was living in Ekfid Twp when she married. Her parents were George and Mary Tanner. (They are error listed as Farmer in the Ancestry files). James and Elizabeth were married in a Methodist Church April 4 1883. As his brother had married a Tanner, the women may have been cousins. On the map of 1878 his property is marked as 50 acres belonging to Mr. Phillips and may have had a cheese factory adjacent.

In 1901 James said he came to Canada in 1856 but in reality it was earlier. Elizabeth said she was born July 22, 1855 in Ingersoll. Their children were William G. born Jan 9 1884, Mary E. July 6 1886, Mabel born Oct 24 1888, Walter J. March 3 1891, John G. Jan 22 1894, Richard Roy June 8 1896.

In 1911 James and family were still at Lot 2 Con 6 Caradoc Twp. Only William was no longer at home. Richard Roy the youngest was 14. James considered himself to be 64 born November 1847 and Elizabeth said she was born July 1857. Two of his brothers William, near London, and George were still living.

In 1921 James and Elizabeth had retired to live on Victoria Street in Strathroy. After he died, I make the assumption that Elizabeth went to live with their son

John who shares their tombstone. No census records after 1921 are yet available.

James died 1924 and was buried at Longwoods Cemetery Caradoc twp. along with his wife Elizabeth Tanner who died in 1950 and son John Gordon 1894 - 1938 and his wife Jean MacKay 1898-1990.

Photo circa 1911 - back - William, Walter,Mary, Gordon. front Elizabeth Tanner Phillips, Roy, Mabel, James Phillips

Richard and Susan Phillips about 1881

More about Richard Phillips.

It appears that Richard, the oldest, lived on a farm at Lot 6 Con 1 Union Road, Dereham. He may have lived there for many years before eventually buying the property. He may have lived on the north half opposite Foldens road although the south half appeared open. On the map of 1876 that south lot is shown without a name. Today there is no building on that lot and on the north half, after the farm was sold, a gravel operation run by the Shelton family was begun. The farm may have been part of the Shuttleworth land but it had several owners while Richard was leasing.

After Richard and Susan Tanner married on Oct 14, 1858, they first lived in Dereham twp., then in West Oxford near Foldens before moving to Dorchester around 1862 where they remained until about 1870. Where exactly was not known. Richard and Susan in 1866 were living in Dorchester Twp when their daughter Elizabeth Jane was born. She died July 10 1887 in Dereham Twp. age 20.

The census of 1871 for Dereham shows Richard 40, Susan 34, William 11, George 9, John Martin 7, Joseph 5, Elizabeth 3 Susan 2 and Richard Edward a new born. (Was this Edwin?) There was a school just down the road to the east and at Duffy road there was a cheese factory for the milk from his cows. This cheese factory was Mr. Ranney's who created with Harris the world's largest cheese in 1866. Thus milk from a Phillips cow may have been in the cheese as it is quite possible he was on the land at that time and the mammoth cheese took a lot of milk. The farm he bought was on Union Road but earlier he may have lived on the next road south.

In 1881 Richard's family had been completed. The ages, it may be noted, are not consistently reported but he was now listed as 50, Susan was 45, William was 21, George was 18, John Martin 16, Elizabeth 12, Richard 10, Martha L. 8, Mary E. 6, and Albert 4. The family of Joe Daniels lived next door and that farm is still in the Daniels family and known as Maple Haven saw mill.

Richard and Susan were able to buy their 100 acre farm, lot 6 Con 1 Dereham in 1882 from John Richardson for $1,500. It was about this time that a family photograph was taken. Where and why is not known but it well may be the celebration of becoming a landowner.

~~~~~~~~~~~~~~~~~~~~~~~~~~~~~~~~~~

Elizabeth 1867, George 1861, John Martin 1863, Joseph James 1865, Susan Ann 1869,
*Richard Edwin1871, William 1860, **Susan 1833, Richard 1830**, Martha 1872,*
Mary Edith 1874, Robert Albert 1875

Photo 1881

In 1891 the census on April 14 said Richard was 68, Susan 54, John 28, Joseph J. 25, Richard E. 20, Martha 19, Mary E. 17 and Albert 14. There was also a hired man from England, Arthur Garthorne, age 26. The family was likely attending the Methodist church at Folden's corners.

Early in 1900 it was reported in the Woodstock Sentinel Review that their youngest daughter Mary E., now about 27, had married Frank Doward of Dereham on Jan 3rd in a quiet wedding in the front room of her parent's residence near Salford. They were married by Rev Johnston of Sweaburg. The couple took the evening train to London.

On March 20th, 1901 Susan, Richard's wife, died. *"Mrs Richard Phillips wife of the prominent farmer living near Peebles died very suddenly yesterday afternoon. Mrs Phillips accompanied by her son-in-law Frank Dorward were driving to the home of her daughter when she suddenly fell back in the cutter and expired. She leaves behind her husband and large family of grown children".* She was buried from Folden's Methodist church at the Ingersoll Rural Cemetery.

At the end of March the census of 1901 reported Richard 72 as a widower. Living with him was John Phillips age 27 and his wife Ellen 23 who had been born in England. John Phillips died June 20, 1902 of erysipelas (blood poisoning) at the Peebles home of Richard who was himself described as very ill. This was not John Martin Phillips. So who was he?

Richard, still on the farm, died May 24 1907 of what was described as anemia. He was 78. The farm was sold.

Richard and Susan's family

Mary Edith/Esther Phillips whose wedding was recounted above was born Jan 5, 1874 and was married to Frank Martin Doward Jan 3, 1900. He was born in England January 24, 1871 and died in 1972. The marriage lasted only about a year and a half when Mary died, perhaps after child birth, August7,1901. Her daughter Blanche was born July 3, 1901. Her mother, Susan, had died suddenly in March 1901.

Richard Edwin Phillips (also Edward) born July 31, 1871 died May 8, 1917 at 8:00 pm at his home lot 11, con 4 in West Oxford. He had been ailing for two years with respiratory failure but was in bed only a week. Besides his wife he left 3 children Howard, Russell, and Wilfred Phillips all at home. He was 46 years old. Services were at Foldens Methodist church.

(There may have been a still born child born 1870 as Richard Edward or it was a typo error)

John Martin Phillips was born Aug 25, 1863 in Dorchester and married Ellen Marwood of East Oxford Twp born 1877 in England on Sept. 6, 1899. He lived most of his life in Dereham but moved to Toronto in 1908 where he died in his 62nd year, June 17, 1924. His sisters Martha and Mary and 4 brothers William, Joseph, and George lived in Ingersoll and Albert lived in Dorchester. His daughters were Elizabeth Phillips and Mrs John Chisholm of Toronto. The funeral was held at his brother-in-law Charlie Hughes home on Wonham St. in Ingersoll. John had been a member of the C.O. F. (Canadian Order of Foresters which was a popular low cost life insurance club) lodge of Folden's Corners.

Joseph James Phillips was born in Dorchester village July 6 or 8, 1865 and after living in Salford he lived in Ingersoll at 82 Bell St. His wife Mary Susan Langstrath Hill whom he married in Seaforth May 24 1893 was originally from Dereham Twp. She was sickly for three years before she died Sept. 24, 1943. He died Nov 9, 1943 a couple of months after his wife and they are buried in Ingersoll Rural Cemetary. Their living children mentioned in their obituary were Clarence of

Belmont, Melvin b.1897 of London, Harry of Ridgetown, Joseph Arthur of Ingersoll, Ethel Beatrice Parrish b. 1900 of St. Thomas, Mary Hudson of Glanworth, Dorah Eveline Minshell (Mitchell?)of Putnam and Mabel Ingram of Ingersoll. Other children were Clive b. 1895, James Richard b. 1898, Edith, Charles Frances. His brother George survived him in Paris ON.

William Phillips born Aug 1, 1859 married Annie Jane Adams. Their son Bruce Phillips owned a grocery store in Ingersoll. Bruce's son was Lloyd. Other children of William were Wallace and Roy.
They lived on Frances St. Ingersoll for 30 years and he worked as a shipper at Ingersoll Packing Company. William died in Ingersoll 23 April 1930 of heart failure. He was a widower.

Martha Lavinia Phillips was born March 1, 1872 and married Charles A. Hughes who died in South Africa in 1943. She died near Durban in South Africa. They lived on her father Richard's farm after his death. Lot 6 con 1 Dereham. Her children were Velma, Olive K, Maurice Gilbert.

Elizabeth Jane Phillips was born October 1866 at Dorchester and died at home in Dereham 10 July 1887.

Susan Ann Phillips born about 1869 and married James Alexander Service at Ingersoll and moved to Listowel in Perth co. where she died Dec 27,1931.

Robert <u>Albert</u> Phillips born Nov 24,1876 in Dereham twp. married Annie Margaret Magee daughter of Isaac Magee and Mary E. Rolston at Putnam ON. She died January 4, 1939 at Putnam, North Dorchester ON. He farmed at Lot B con B North Dorchester. Albert died Oct 16, 1932 of infection after appendix removal.

George Phillips

Grandson of William and Elizabeth and son of Richard and Susan Tanner was born 1861 and grew up at the farm in Peebles, lot 6 con 1 Dereham Twp. Today it is Union Rd. He was a tall thin boy.

George married Martha Louise Tanner at Appin on April 20, 1887. Her father was George Tanner of Ekfrid Township. George Tanner had come to Canada with his brother Martin and sister Susan from Ring Hill near Dury farm in Lydford. So Martha Louise was in fact George Phillips cousin as his father Richard had married George Tanner's sister Susan. Martha LouiseTanner was born February 27, 1869. In 1881 her family at home with her were father George 47, mother Mary A. 44 , Elizabeth 23, George 21, William 19, Joseph 17, Martin 15, Llewellyn (Lew) 8, (born Aug 1 1872-died Nov 25 1947 buried in Michigan Memorial Park), Mary Ellen 6. The Tanner farm was in Ekfrid next to Caradoc Twp.

In 1891 George and Martha were living on a farm in West Oxford. Stanley, their son, was born September 18,1887 in Dereham twp. Myrtle was born Feb 15, 1889. Ten years later in the new century 1901 George was working as a laborer and living on John St. Ingersoll where he was earning 360 dollars a year, a sum which was larger than most his neighbors were earning. However that work was for 60 hours a week which was normal. George stated that he was born January 6,1863 but he was recorded earlier as born in March of 1861. His son, Stanley, age 12, had just died presumably of diphtheria, a childhood illness. The local paper said " The sympathy of the towns people will be extended to Mr. And Mrs. George Phillips, John Street, on the loss of their 12 year old son, Stanley whose death occured on Thursday after a few days illness with diptheria." Fri. March 29 1901.

Stanley's sisters Myrtle and Edna born Oct 26, 1891 were joined by Albert Lorne Phillips April 26, 1905. Edna Mae married Thomas Parker on October 26, 1908 and lived in West Zorra Twp.(Embro). Dorothy Phillips was born to Myrtle May 1, 1910 and raised by her parents George and Martha whose last child was Donald Truman Phillips born January 24,1912. Donald was unaware that Dorothy was his cousin and not his sister until he was well into adulthood, likely after 1950. In 1911 George was working at the Morrow Bolt factory in Ingersoll where the company made bicycle parts and machine screws and nuts from iron and brass. He was a bolt maker. He was making $450.00 dollars a year and still working 58 hours a week. It is unclear whether he was represented in a company photo taken in 1909 as he began work there about 1893. Myrtle married Earnest Frederick Scott on 23 July 23, 1912. In 1914 Fred joined the army.

George, Martha, Dorothy 11, Lorne 16 and Donald 9 in 1921 lived on Helen Street which ran from Mutual to King Solomon St. but the street no longer exists. There is one house on Helen where it meets King Solomon. George worked as a machinist but his wages had increased considerably and they owned their own home in Ingersoll. In the Canada census of 1921 the name was Philipps.

George and Martha moved to 111 Bay St. Woodstock in 1928 where he worked for the Woodstock Rubber Company after having worked at John Morrow Screw and Nut in Ingersoll for 35 years. When Martha died May 29, 1945 after two years of failing health, George went to live with his son Lorne in Brantford where George died January 26, 1947.

Martha L. Tanner and George attended Old St. Paul's Anglican church. She was survived by daughters Myrtle F. Scott of Walter street Woodstock, Dorothy Sanders and by two sons Lorne of Brantford and Donald of Paris. There were 9 grandchildren and 9 great grandchildren. Two sisters survived her - Mrs. Bert Patterson of London and Mrs. Lizzie Phillips of London and also 3 brothers Lew Tanner of Detroit, George Tanner of Mt. Brydges and Joe Tanner of Melbourne. Interment was in the Anglican Cemetery.

https://www.familysearch.org/ark:/61903/2:2:3B47-298   has a summary

George and Martha Phillips about 1940

Mary Ann Scott in arms of Fred, Myrtle. **George**, *Dorothy, Donald, Lorne and* **Martha**. Photo late 1914 or early 2015

The Descendants Record of William and Elizabeth

All of the genealogic records for the descendants are printed in the following pages with some comments about the families. This info may not be completely accurate. In many cases family member information was not known. Census records and FamilySearch.org records are used. It is possible to add additional information by adding your own notes or passing material along to the author to be incorporated into another edition. As mentioned before, this book is an on demand print and can easily be altered. The material below is as known up until the date of publication in June 2021. The material was recorded first in the Family Tree (version 12) data base. The documentation that follows is a descendants report from that program. In converting line spacing, indentation, script and other set up, information was altered and although much was corrected, some of the set up may still be variable.

The superscript ^{1} in a name indicates the generation from William ^{1} and appears only in the name of the first born of a family.

The first number is a serial listing. By following the link of Person 33 you will be able to find 33 farther in the list again if there were children. For an individual the children are shown as i, ii, etc. After the original list newly added names are usually added with the next sequential ID number. In that case they will seem mixed up (example 71,72, 341, 73)

The known descendants of William and Elizabeth now number about 350 and go at least to 6 generations.

More Notes

Descendants of William Phillips

1. WILLIAM¹ PHILLIPS was born in 1799 in Lydford, England. He died on 28 Sep 1864 in Ingersoll Ontario. He married Elizabeth Waldon on 11 Jan 1829. She was born in 1799 in Lydford England. She died on 20 Nov 1883 in Longwood Station, Middlesex, ON.

Generation 1

William Phillips and Elizabeth Waldon had the following children:

2. i. RICHARD² PHILLIPS was born on 20 Feb 1829 in Dury Farm, Postbridge, Lydford, Devon, England. He died on 24 May 1907 in Dereham Twp ON buried Ingersoll, On. He married Susannah Tanner, daughter of George Tanner and Elizabeth Davis on 14 Oct 1858 in Dereham Twp ON. She was born in 1835 in Ring hill farm, Postbridge, Lydford, England. She died in 1901 in Dereham Twp ON.

3. ii. WILLIAM PHILLIPS was born on 15 Nov 1830 in Dury, Lydford, Devonshire, England. He died on 27 Feb 1918 and buried in St. John's cemetery Arva, On.. He married Francis Burtch, daughter of Benjamin Burtch and Anna, on 04 Mar 1863 in Woodstock, Ontario. She was born on 12 Aug 1841 in Ireland. She died on 07 Nov 1915 in Arva, ON.

4. iii. MARY E. PHILLIPS was born in 1833 in Dury Farm, Lydford Devonshire, England. She died on 02 Dec 1897 in St. George ON. She married John Richardson, son of Peter Richardson and Elizabeth Foster, on 25 Nov 1861 in Ingersoll ON. He was born in 1833 in Yorkshire, England. He died on 26 May 1896 in St. George ON.

5.   iv. GEORGE PHILPS (see pg. 55)was born in 1835 in Dury Lydford, Devonshire, England. He died on 09 Jan 1886 in Longwood Caradoc twp Middlesex co Ontario. He married Ellen Hamlin, daughter of Elias Hamlin and Susan on 13 Nov 1861 in Woodstock, Ontario. She was born in 1841.

6.   v. GRACE PHILLIPS was born on 18 Mar 1840 in Dury, Lydford, Devonshire , England. She died in 1904 in Longwood Caradoc twp Middlesex co Ontario. She married Francis Atkinson, son of Christopher Atkinson and Frances, on 04 Mar 1863. He was born in 1834 in Cumberland, England. He died on 30 Jul 1917 in Longwood Caradoc Middlesex co Ontario.

7.   vi. JOHN PHILLIPS was born on 07 Jan 1841 in Devonshire , England. He died on 15 Jul 1909 in Watertown, South Dakota. He married Tabitha Taylor on 24 Dec 1868 in Ingersoll ON. She was born in 1847 in England. She died on 09 Sep 1914 in Watertown SD.

8.   vii. JAMES F. PHILLIPS was born on 1840 (1841) in Dury farm, Lydford, Devonshire, England. He died on 16 Jan 1924 in Longwoods Caradoc twp Middlesex co ON. He married ELIZABETH ANN TANNER. She was born on 22 Jul 1856 in Ingersoll Ontario . She died on 08 Apr 1950.

Generation 2

2. RICHARD[2] PHILLIPS (William[1]) was born on 20 Feb 1829 in Dury Farm, Postbridge, Lydford, Devon, England. He died on 24 May 1907 in Dereham Twp ON buried Ingersoll,ON. He married Susannah Tanner, daughter of George Tanner and Elizabeth Davis on 14 Oct 1858 in Dereham Twp ON. She was born in 1835 in Ring hill farm, Postbridge, Princetown, Lydford , England. She died in 1901 in Dereham Twp ON.

Richard Phillips and Susannah Tanner had the following children:

9.   i. WILLIAM[3] PHILLIPS was born on 01 Aug 1859 in Dereham Twp ON. He died on 23 Apr 1930 in Ingersoll ON. He married Annie Jane Adams. She was born in 1865 in West Oxford ON. She died on 08 Jan 1925 in Oxford co ON. Her parents were George Adam and Georgina McPherson. William was a Presbyterian and worked at a packing company in Ingersoll.

10.   ii. JOHN MARTIN PHILLIPS was born on 25 Aug 1863 in Dorchester ON. He died on 17 Jun 1924 in Toronto ON. He married Ellen Marwood, daughter of Walter Marwood and Sarah Stockman on 06 Sep 1899. She was born on 28 Apr 1877 in Devon, England. She died on 20 Jun 1902 in Dereham Twp ON.

11.   iii. ELIZABETH PHILLIPS was born in 1866. She died on 10 July 1887 in Ingersoll.

12.   iv. JOSEPH J. PHILLIPS was born on 06 Jul 1865 in Dorchester ON. He died on 09 Nov 1943 in Ingersoll ON. He married Mary Susan Hill

on 24 May 1893 in Seaforth, Huron, Ontario, . She was born in 1869. She died in 1943 in Ingersoll ON.

13. Does not exist due to an error.

14.   v. ANN PHILLIPS (also Anna or Annie) was born in 1869. She died on 27 Dec 1931 in Ingersoll ON. She married J. Alexander Service of Tillsonburg ON at Ingersoll on Jan 29, 1890. The Service family farmed in north east Dereham twp.

15.   vi. RICHARD EDWIN PHILLIPS was born in 1871. He died on 08 May 1917 in West Oxford ON. He married MONTALENA HILL. Edwin and Monta were married 11 Oct. 1893 at West Oxford. She was born Jan 22 1875. She died on 25 Sep 1957.

16.   vii. MARTHA PHILLIPS was born in 1872 in Dereham Twp ON. She died in 1943 in Durban, South Africa. She married CHARLES A HUGHES. He was born in 1870. He died in 1943 in Durban, South Africa.

17.   viii, MARY E. PHILLIPS was born in 1874. She died on 07 Aug 1901 in Dereham Twp ON. She married Frank Martin Doward on 03 Jan 1900. He was born on 24 Jan 1871 in England. He died in 1972.

18.   ix. ALBERT PHILLIPS was born in 1875 in Salford, ON. He died on 16 Oct 1932 in Ingersoll, ON. He married Annie Margaret Magee on 04 Oct 1899. She was born on 30 May 1875. She died on 04 Jan 1039.

19.   x. GEORGE PHILLIPS was born on 06 Mar 1861 in Dereham Twp ON. He died on 26 Jan 1947 in Brantford ON. He married MARTHA LOUISE TANNER. She was born on 27 Feb 1869 in Melbourne, Ekfrid ON. She died on 29 May 1945 in Woodstock Ontario .

3. WILLIAM² PHILLIPS (William¹) was born on 15 Nov 1830 in Dury, Lydford, Devonshire England. He died on 27 Feb 1918 in St. John's cemetery Arva On.. He married Francis Burtch, daughter of Benjamin Burtch and Anna on 04 Mar 1863 in Woodstock Ontario . She was born on 12 Aug 1841 in Ireland. She died on 07 Nov 1915 in Arva, ON

William Phillips and Francis Burtch had the following children:

20   i.   SARAH ANNE³ PHILLIPS was born in 1862 in London twp, Middlesex county as were all her siblings listed below, 21 to 27.

21   ii.   FRANCIS EDWIN PHILLIPS was born in 1864.

22   iii.   WILLIAM BENJAMIN PHILLIPS was born in 1866.

23   iv.   CHARLES HERBERT PHILLIPS was born in 1869.

24   v.   ALBERT HENRY PHILLIPS was born in Nov 1870.

25   vi.   WALTER JAMES PHILLIPS was born in 1876. He married SARAH SHOEBOTTOM. She was born in 1880.

26   vii.   JOHN PHILLIPS was born in Jan 1881 in London twp, Middlesex Co. On. He died before 1890.

27   viii.   MABLE PHILLIPS was born in 1885.

4. MARY E.² PHILLIPS (William¹) was born in 1833 in Dury Farm, Lydford Devonshire , England. She died on 02 Dec 1897 in St. George ON. She married John Richardson, son of Peter Richardson and Elizabeth Foster on 25 Nov 1861 in Ingersoll ON. He was born in 1833 in Yorkshire, England. He died on 26 May 1896 in St. George ON.

John Richardson and Mary E. Phillips had the following children:

28   i.   ELIZABETH ANN[3] RICHARDSON was born on 22 Apr 1870 in St. George ON

29   ii.   PETER RICHARDSON was born in 1867 in St. George ON. He died about 1872 in St. George ON.

30   iii.   PETER THOMAS RICHARDSON was born on 25 May 1873 in St. George ON

31   iv.   WILLIAM RICHARDSON was born in 1868 in St. George ON.

32   v.   ANN PHILIP RICHARDSON was born in 1869 in St. George ON.

33   vi.   ROBERT RICHARDSON was born in 1871 in St. George ON.

~~~~~~~~~~~~~~~~~~~~

5.   GEORGE[2] PHILPS (William[1] Phillips) was born in 1835 in Dury Lydford, Devonshire , England. He died on 09 Jan 1886 in Longwood Caradoc Middlesex co Ontario. He married Ellen Hamlin, daughter of Elias Hamlin and Susan on 13 Nov 1861 in Woodstock, Ontario, . She was born in 1841. Note: his name was Philps

George Philps and Ellen Hamlin had the following children:

34   i.   JAMES[3] PHILPS was born in 1861 in Embro ON West Zorra twp. He died in Strathroy, Middlesex, Ontario, .

35   ii.   WALTER PHILPS was born in 1863 in Embro ON West Zorra twp. He died on 04 Feb 1907 in Longwood Caradoc Middlesex co Ontario. NOT MARRIED. He was killed at a train crossing in horse and buggy.

36   iii.   THOMAS PHILPS was born in 1865 in Embro ON West Zorra

twp. He married ALICIA EMMALINE RICHARDS. She was born in 1872. She died in 1970 in Longwood Caradoc Middlesex co Ontario

37   iv.   ALBERT   PHILPS was born on 15 Sep 1868 in Embro ON West Zorra twp. He died in Caradoc township ,Ontario. He married Mary Warren, daughter of Henry Warren and Mary Hirshman on 28 May 1897 in Caradoc Township Ontario. She was born in 1870 in Adelaide Twp Middlesex co ON. She died on 03 Sep 1951 in Longwood Caradoc Middlesex co Ontario.

~~~~~~~~~~~~~~~~~~

6.   GRACE[2] PHILLIPS (William[1]) was born on 18 Mar 1840 in Dury, Lydford, Devonshire , England. She died in 1904 in Longwood Caradoc Middlesex co Ontario. She married Francis Atkinson, son of Christopher Atkinson and Frances on 04 Mar 1863. He was born in 1834 in Cumberland, England. He died on 30 Jul 1917 in Longwood Caradoc Middlesex co Ontario.   Notes for Francis Atkinson:The Walker/Younker family tree on Ancestry.com has descendants of this family particularly the Gowanlock and other Atkinsons.

Francis Atkinson and Grace Phillips had the following children:

38   i.   CHRISTOPHER[3] ATKINSON was born in 1864 in Ontario.

39   ii.   JAMES ATKINSON was born in 1864 in Middlesex co Ontario. He died in 1881 in Middlesex co Ontario.

40   iii. HENRY ATKINSON was born in 1868 in Embro ON West Zorra twp. He married Elizabeth Langdon on 12 Jun 1899 in Toronto.

41   iv.   FRANCIS [I] ATKINSON was born in 1870 in Middlesex co Ontario. She died in 1925. She married WILLIAM GOWANLOCK. He was born in 1857.

42   v.   WILLIAM ATKINSON was born in 1871 in Oxford co ON. He died in 1924 in Ingersoll ON. He married ERMINA PIPER. She was born in

1871.

43   vi. ELIZABETH ATKINSON was born in 1872 in Oxford co ON. She married WALTER SHIERS. He was born in 1874.

44   vii. ROBERT ATKINSON was born in 1876 in Middlesex co Ontario. He died in 1934.

45   viii. CHARLES ATKINSON was born in 1878. He died in 1930 in Ingersoll ON. He married ELSIE MAE LANGDON. She was born in 1885.

46   ix. MARY ELLEN ATKINSON was born in 1880 in Caradoc township Ontario. Notes for Mary Ellen Atkinson: known as Fanny (census 1901)

47   x. GEORGE ATKINSON was born in 1882. He died on 17 Jun 1935 in Lambton co ON. He married OLA FOWLER. She was born in 1891.

48   xi. JAMES EDGAR ATKINSON was born in 1885. James Edgar died in 1908 in Middlesex co Ontario.

~~~~~~~~~~~~~~~~~~~~~~~~~~~~~~~

7.   JOHN[2] PHILLIPS (William[1]) was born on 07 Jan 1841 in Devonshire He died on 15 Jul 1909 in Watertown, SD. He married Tabitha Taylor on 24 Dec 1868 in Ingersoll ON. She was born in 1847 in England. She died on 09 Sep 1914 in Watertown SD.

John Phillips and Tabitha Taylor had the following children:

49   i. CHARLES[3] PHILLIPS was born in 1869 in Dereham Twp ON.

50   ii. WILLIAM GORDON PHILLIPS was born on 05 Apr 1881 in South Dorchester Middlesex Co ON.

51   iii. FREDERICK PHILLIPS was born in 1878 in South Dorchester Middlesex .

52   iv. NETTIE MAY PHILLIPS was born in 1879. She died in 1882.

53   v.   LOUIS AMELIA PHILLIPS was born in Sep 1874 in South Dorchester Middlesex Co ON. She married WILLIAM JESSE MINOR. He was born in Wisconsin, USA. He died in 1896 in Watertown, SD. She married ALBERT CHRISTIAN.

54   vi.   EARL DEWAYNE PHILLIPS was born in Aug 1892 in Watertown SD. He died in 1962.

~~~~~~~~~~~~~~~~~~~~~~~~~~~~

8.   JAMES F.[2] PHILLIPS (William[1]) was born on 1840 (1841) in Dury farm, Lydford, Devonshire , England. He died on 16 Jan 1924 in Longwoods Caradoc twp Middlesex co ON. He married ELIZABETH ANN TANNER. She was born on 22 Jul 1856 in Ingersoll Ontario . She died on 08 Apr 1950.

James F. Phillips and Elizabeth Ann Tanner had the following children:

55   i.   WILLIAM GEORGE[3] PHILLIPS wasborn on 09 Jan 1884 in Metcalfe. Middlesex county. He died in 1964 in London Ontario . He married ELIZA ANNIE BLAIR. She was born in 1893.

56   ii. MARY ELIZABETH PHILLIPS was born on 06 Jul 1886 in Caradoc township Ontario. She died   Feb 24, 1962 in London,ON. She married WILLIAM DAVID REYNOLDS. He was born in 1887. He died October 3, 1926.

57   iii. MABEL ELLEN PHILLIPS was born on 24 Oct 1888 in Caradoc twp ON. She died on 12 Mar 1970 in Strathroy ON. She married William Allen Ballentine son of James Ballantine and Nancy McDougall on 26 Aug 1915. He was born on 08 Apr 1887 in   Caradoc township ON. He died on 26 Dec 1976 in ON.

58.   iv. WALTER JAMES PHILLIPS was born on 03 Mar 1891 in Caradoc township ON. He died on 27 Oct 1940 in ON. He married (1) MAY WALTERS in Sep 1921. She died on 03 May 1925. He married (2) MARGARET HENNERMAN on 15 Aug 1931.

59   v. JOHN GORDON PHILLIPS was born on 22 Jan 1894 in Caradoc township ON. He died on 06 Jun 1939 in Caradoc township ON. He married JEAN McKAY. She was born in 1898. She died on 13 Feb 1990 in Caradoc township ON.

60.   vi. RICHARD ROY PHILLIPS was born on 08 Jun 1896 in Caradoc township ON. He died on 17 Oct 1956 in Strathroy, ON. He married Gladys Beattie on 10 Feb 1920. She was born on 08 Jun 1897. She died on 05 Aug 1980 in Strathroy ON.

Generation 3

9. WILLIAM[3] PHILLIPS (Richard[2], William[1]) was born on 01 Aug 1859 in Dereham twp. He died on 23 Apr 1930 in Ingersoll ON. He married ANNIE JANE ADAMS. She was born in 1865 in West Oxford ON. She died on 08 Jan 1925 in Oxford co. They were married at St. John's Ingersoll June 4 1884. Her parents were George and Georgina Adams.

William Phillips and Annie Jane Adams had the following children:

61 i. RICHARD BRUCE[4] PHILLIPS was born on 30 Sep 1884 in ON. He died in 1960. He married Gertrude Turner on 30 Oct 1917. She was born June 23 1886 in England. Died Mar 3 1946. Bruce died Feb 14 1961 (Ingersoll Rural) He ran a grocery store on Thames St , lived above the store and later farmed at Folden's Corner. In 1953 moved to lot 28 B.F. Con of West Oxford. Gertrude came to alone at age 10 and lived with George Beck. Parents were Samuel Turner and Hannah Ward. She was possibly a Dr. Bernardo relocation child.

62 ii. GEORGE ROYAL PHILLIPS was born in 1866 in ON.He died in 1957. He married MARY MARGARET BERDAN. She was born in 1887 in Bayham township. She died on 05 Mar 1933 in Oxford co. ON.

63 iii. WALLACE ADAM PHILLIPS was born in 1894 in Oxford co. ON. He died in 1960 in Oxford co ON. He married CORRIE AURELIA KNEAL.

~~~~~~~~~~~~~~~~~~~~~~~~~~~~~~~

10. JOHN MARTIN[3] PHILLIPS (Richard[2], William[1]) was born on 25 Aug 1863 in Dorchester ON. He died on 17 Jun 1924 in Toronto ON. He married Ellen Marwood, daughter of Walter Marwood and Sarah Stockman on 06 Sep 1899. She was born on 28 Apr 1877 in Devon, England. She died on 20 Jun 1902 in Dereham Twp ON.

John Martin Phillips and Ellen Marwood had the following children:

64   i   VERA MAY PHILLIPS was born on 09 May 1900 in Ingersoll ON. She died in 1988. She had a spouse and children.

65   ii. ELIZABETH LOUISE PHILLIPS was born on 20 Nov 1901 in Oxford co. She died in Nov 1987 in Orillia, Simcoe, ON, Canada. She married ROBERT PONTON. He was born on 02 Jun 1899 in Edinburgh Scotland. He died on 16 Nov 1968 in Newmarket ON.

~~~~~~~~~~~~~~~~~~~~~~~~~~~~~~~

12   JOSEPH JAMES[3] PHILLIPS (Richard[2], William[1]) was born on 06 July 1865 in Dorchester ON. He died on   09 Nov 1943 at 62 Bell St., Ingersoll ON. He married Mary Susan Hill on (age 24) 24 May 1893 at Seaforth, Huron, ON, Canada. She was born in Aug 1869 in Dereham twp. She died in 1943 in Ingersoll ON. In 1911 Joseph, a methodist, was farming at lot 10 Con 11 East Nissouri Twp. Oxford county.

Joseph James Phillips and Mary Susan Hill had the following children:
66   i.   CLARENCE[4] PHILLIPS born Feb 1894
341   ii. CLIVE PHILLIPS born Aug 1 1895 died 7 Dec 1914
342   iii. MELVIN PHILLIPS born 1897 in East Oxford Twp.
343   iv. JAMES R. PHILLIPS born April 1899
344   v.   ETHEL PHILLIPS born Aug 1900
69   vi. MARY E. PHILLIPS. Born Sept 1902 married a Hudson
67   vii. HARRY M. PHILLIPS. Born Oct 1904
68   viii. JOSEPH ARTHUR PHILLIPS born 1 Oct 1906 West Oxford
70   ix. DORA EVELINE PHILLIPS born 1 Oct 1906 West Oxford
346   xi. EDITH PHILLIPS born June 3, 1908
71   xii. MABEL PHILLIPS born June 3, 1908
347   xiii. CHARLES F. PHILLIPS born 1910

~~~~~~~~~~~~~~~~~~~~~~~~~~~~~

15   RICHARD EDWIN[3] PHILLIPS (Richard[2], William[1]) was born July

31, 1871in Dereham Twp. He died on 08 May 1917 in West Oxford ON. He married MONTALENA HILL. She was born in 1875. She died on 25 Sept 1957. Both buried Ingersoll Rural. Edwin and Monta were married 11 Oct. 1893 at West Oxford

Richard Edwin Phillips and Montalena Hill had the following children:

72 i. JAMES HOWARD⁴ PHILLIPS. born 19 June 1902 died 30 June 1955

73 ii. EDWIN RUSSELL PHILLIPS. born 11 Nov 1905 died 4 Mar 1983

Russell and Mabel operated a grocery store at 267 Dundas st. just south of Delatre St. Woodstock from before 1938 until at least 1964. He married Mabel McIntyre (1909-1995) and lived above the store. Their child was :

338 Lois Anne Phillips 1945-2016 (Generation 4) who married Richard MacKay Crotty.

74 iii. ALVIN WILFRED PHILLIPS, b. 23 Aug 1908

~~~~~~~~~~~~~~~~~~~~~~~~~~~~~~~

16 MARTHA³ PHILLIPS (Richard², William¹) was born in 1872 in Dereham Twp ON. She died in 1943 in Durban, South Africa. She married CHARLES A. HUGHES. He was born in 1870. He died in 1943 in Durban, South Africa. Martha Phillips was buried in Denby SA. In 1911 they were living on the farm owned by her late father Richard. They had 2 domestic help and a teacher Mabel Gilbert boarding with them.

Charles A Hughes and Martha Phillips had the following children:

75 i VELMA⁴ HUGHES born June 1895 She married WILLIAM R SAGE. He was born in 1894 in West Oxford. He died in 1942 in Ingersoll.

339   ii   OLIVE K. HUGHES Born Nov 1897

340   iii MAURICE GILBERT HUGHES born 02 July 1909 also spelled Morris. He died June 30 1980 at Ingersoll ON, buried in Harris St. Cemetery.

<hr />

17   MARY ESTHER[3] PHILLIPS (Richard[2], William[1]) was born in 1874. She died on 07 Aug 1901 in Dereham Twp ON. She married Frank Martin Doward on 03 Jan 1900. He was born on 24 Jan 1871 in England. He died in 1972.

Frank Martin Doward and Mary E. Phillips had the following child:

76   i. C. BLANCHE[4] DOWARD was born on 03 Jul 1901 in Oxford co ON. She married HAROLD SWANCE.

<hr />

18A.   ALBERT[3] PHILLIPS (Richard[2], William[1]) was born 24 Nov 1876 in Salford, ON. He died on 16 Oct 1932 in Ingersoll ON. He married Annie Margaret Magee daughter of Issac McGee on 04 Oct 1899. She was born on 30 May 1875. She died on 04 Jan 1939. Albert farmed lot B con B North Dorchester.

Notes for Albert Phillips: may have died in Dorchester

Albert Phillips and Annie Margaret Magee had the following children:

77   i.   LEO AMERSON   PHILLIPS. Born 1 Nov 1900, married Christine Cooper born 1899.

78   ii.   WILLARD[4] EARL PHILLIPS born Sept 1904 died 1971 married Thelma Benjamin 1919 - 2008

79   iii. GLADYS PHILLIPS born 1910

Albert and Annie also had Frank 1907-8, Fred 1907-9, Jesse Albert born 19 Nov 1912

~~~~~~~~~~~~~~~~~~~~~~~~~~~~

19.   GEORGE[3] PHILLIPS (Richard[2], William[1]) was born on 06 Mar 1861 in Dereham Twp ON. He died on 26 Jan 1947 in Brantford ON. He married MARTHA LOVINIA TANNER. She was born on 27 Feb 1869 in Ekfrid ON. She died on 29 May 1945 in 111 Bay st., Woodstock ON. Her parents were George and Mary Ann Tanner. (See page 20)

George Phillips and Martha Tanner had the following children:

80   i.   STANLEY ARNOLD PHILLIPS was born on 18 Sep 1887 in Dereham Twp ON. He died in 1901 of diptheria at Ingersoll.

81   ii.   MYRTLE JANE PHILLIPS was born 15 February 1890 in Dereham Twp ON. She died 29 Jan 1965 in Woodstock ON.She married Ernest FRED SCOTT. He was born on 17 Dec 1888 in Eaton Norfolk England. They were married 23 of July 1912 in Woodstock ON. He died in Sep 1958 in Woodstock ON.

82   iii. EDNA MAE PHILLIPS was born on 26 Oct 1891 in west Oxford twp Oxford county. She died on 20 Jan 1923 in Embro ON. She married Thomas William Parker on 26 Oct 1908 in Ingersoll ON Canada. He was born on 21 Jan 1886 in East Zorra ON. He died on 05 Aug 1973 in Embro ON.

83   iv JOHN GEORGE PHILLIPS was born in Feb 1902 in Ingersoll ON. He died in 1902.

84   v. ALBERT LORNE PHILLIPS was born on 26 April 1905 in West Oxford twp., Oxford county. He died July 18 1967 in Brantford ON. He

married Hilda Augusta Amanda Maria Rasmussen on 24 Dec 1931 in Woodstock ON. She was born in Oct 1906.

85   vi. WILLIAM ARNOLD PHILLIPS was born in 1909 in Ingersoll ON. He died in 1909.

86   vii. DOROTHY MAE PHILLIPS was born on 01 May 1910 in Ingersoll ON Canada. She died on 31 Jan 1994 in Embro ON West Zorra twp. She married Alexander James Sanders on 11 Jul 1929 in Woodstock ON. He was born on 18 Oct 1909 in Embro ON West Zorra twp. He died on 13 Jul 1977 in Embro ON West Zorra twp. Dorothy was the biological child of Myrtle but raised as the daughter of George and Martha. Dorothy is Generation 5 not 4.

87   viii. DONALD TRUMAN PHILLIPS was born on 24 Jan 1912 in Ingersoll ON Canada. He died on 25 Jun 1974 in Woodstock ON. He married Margaret Martindale on 05 Oct 1939 in Paris ON Canada. She was born on 18 Jul 1910 in Darwin Lancashire England and lived on Dumfries St., Paris. She died on 04 Jan 1973 , Main st., Woodstock ON.

~~~~~~~~~~~~~~~~~~~~~~~~~~~~~~

17.   THOMAS^3 PHILPS (George^2, William^1 Phillips) was born in 1865 in Embro ON West Zorra twp. He married ALECIA EMALINE RICHARDS. She was born in 1872. She died in 1970 in Longwood Caradoc Middlesex co

Thomas Philps and Alecia Emaline Richards had the following child:

88   i. WINSTON RICHARD^4 PHILPS.

~~~~~~~~~~~~~~~~~~~~~~~~~~~~~~

18B.   ALBERT^3 PHILPS (George^2, William^1 Phillips) was born on 15 Sep 1868 in Embro ON West Zorra twp. He died in Caradoc township ON. He married Mary Warren, daughter of Henry Warren and Mary Hirshman on 28 May 1897 in Caradoc township ON. She was born in 1870 in Adelaide Twp Middlesex co ON. She died on 03 Sep 1951 in Longwood Caradoc Middlesex co ON.

Albert Philps and Mary Warren had the following children:

89   i.   ROSE^4 PHILPS was born in 1900 in Caradoc township ON. She died in 1973 in Longwood Caradoc Middlesex co ON. She married GEORGE SEBURN. He was born in 1883. He died in 1953 in Longwood Caradoc Middlesex co ON

90   ii.   GLADYS PHILPS. She married GEORGE OLDE.

91   iii.   GEORGE PHILPS.

92   iv.   WARREN PHILPS was born in 1913 in Caradoc township ON. He died on Nov. 17 1982 in Longwood Caradoc Middlesex co ON. He married ALICE KELLERSTEIN. She was born in 1917. She died in 2005 in Longwood Caradoc Middlesex co ON.

19   LOUISE AMELIA^3 PHILLIPS (John^2, William^1) was born in Sep 1874 in South Dorchester Middlesex Co ON. She married WILLIAM JESSE MINOR. He was born in Wisconsin, USA. He died in 1896 in Watertown, SD. She married ALBERT CHRISTIAN.
She died in 1930.

William Jesse Minor and Louise Amelia Phillips had the following children:

93   i.   JESSE PITTMAN^4 MINOR was born in Sep 1894 in Watertown, SD. He died in 1964. He married AMY CONTENT TRENHOLM. She was

born in 1895. She died in 1976.

94   ii. WILLIAM TAYLOR MINOR was born in Oct 1895 in Watertown, SD. He died in 1976. He married RUTH.

20.   WILLIAM GEORGE[3] PHILLIPS (James F.[2], William[1]) was born on 09 Jan 1884 in Metcalfe twp. Middlesex Co. He died in 1964 in London, ON He married ELIZA ANNIE BLAIR. She was born in 1893.

William George Phillips and Eliza Annie Blair children:

140   i. HAZEL MARIE[4] PHILLIPS was born on 13 Jun 1914.

95   ii. LILLIAN JEAN PHILLIPS was born on 23 Apr 1916 in Caradoc township ON. She married Hugh Leslie Walker on 05 Jul 1941.

96   iii. WALTER BLAIR PHILLIPS was born on 06 May 1918 in Caradoc township ON. He died on 05 Jan 1989 in London ON. He married Margaret Joan Dagg on 15 Jul 1954 in London ON. She was born on 14 Oct 1922 in Kamsack, Saskatchewan, Canada. She died on 01 Aug 1989 in London ON.

21.   MARY ELIZABETH[3] PHILLIPS (James F.[2], William[1]) was born on 06 Jul 1886 in Caradoc township ON. She died in 1962 in London,ON. She married WILLIAM DAVID REYNOLDS in 1912. born in 1887.

William David Reynolds and Mary Elizabeth Phillips had the following children:

97   i. MABEL ELIZABETH[4] REYNOLDS was born on 02 Feb 1913 in London, ON She died on 29 Oct 1981 in London ON. She married Douglas Leader Slemmon on 26 Aug 1939 in Melbourne Caradoc twp. He was born on 25 Mar 1913 in London ON. He died on 17 Nov 1993 in London ON.

149   ii.   ETHEL BEATRICE REYNOLDS was born on 14 Jun 1914. She died on 22 Feb 1918.

98   iii.   JAMES WILLIAM REYNOLDS was born on 16 Feb 1916 in Alisa Craig, Middlesex cty, On. He died on 19 July 1959 in London ON. He married Gwendolyn Ethel Ruth Mountenay on 21 Aug 1943 in Tillsonburg, Oxford, ON, Canada. She was born on 13 Oct 1924 in Omeemee, Victoria cty. Ruth died Nov 27, 2003

Reynolds - Phillips wedding -Elizabeth Philips, James, Elizabeth on right   William David Reynolds, his family on left

99   iv.   JOHN HOWARD REYNOLDS was born on 13 Nov 1917 in London ON. He married Nora Emily Harris on 29 Jun 1946 in London ON. She was born on 01 Nov 1922 in London ON. Howard died March 14, 2007.

Nora died Sept 21, 2018

100   v.   GORDON ALFRED REYNOLDS was born on 21 Apr 1920 in Hensall, Huron, ON, Canada. He married Alma Noreen Howe on 14 Aug 1948 in London ON. She was born on 22 Sep 1925 in London ON. Gordon died Sept. 21, 2004

101   vi. CLIFFORD STANLEY REYNOLDS was born on 18 Nov 1921 in London ON. He died on 18 Nov 1998 in London ON. He married Mary Isabelle Jacobs on 10 Feb 1945 in London ON. She was born on 21 Jul 1927. He died on his birthday 1998.

102   vii. CORA PEARL REYNOLDS was born on 30 May 1923 in London ON. Died Oct 3, 2016

103   viii. EVELYN MARY REYNOLDS was born on 05 Dec 1924 in London ON. Died Jan 31, 2021

104   ix. VERNON CYRUS REYNOLDS was born on 22 Mar 1926 in London ON. He married Helen Jean Walker on 10 Jun 1950 in London ON. She was born on 01 Jul 1927 in London ON.

~~~~~~~~~~~~~~~~~~~~~~~~~~~~~

22   MABEL ELLEN[3] PHILLIPS (James F.[2], William[1]) was born on 24 Oct 1888 in Caradoc township ON. She died on 12 Mar 1970 in Strathroy ON. She married William Allen Ballantine, son of James Ballantine and Nancy McDougall on 26 Aug 1915. He was born on 08 Apr 1887 in Caradoc township ON. He died on 26 Dec 1976 in ON. Notes for Mabel Ellen Phillips: she may have had another daughter who married Robert James Steep born 1923 and died 2008.

William Allen Ballantine and Mabel Ellen Phillips had the following children:

105   i.   DONALD JAMES[4] BALLANTINE was born on 15 Jun 1916 in Caradoc township ON. He died on 16 Aug 1985 in Mt Brydges,ON. He married Doris Cobban in 1947 in Caradoc township ON. She was born on 08 Oct 1920.

106.   ii. DOROTHY ISABEL BALLANTINE was born on 15 Jan 1922. She died on 07 Oct 1998 in   Mt. Brydges,ON. She married HARRY STINSON MCCRAKEN. He was born in 1916.

107   iii.   MARION ELIZABETH BALLANTINE was born on 16 Aug 1925. She married ROBERT STEEPE.

~~~~~~~~~~~~~~~~~~~~~~~~~~~~~~~

23   WALTER JAMES[3] PHILLIPS (James F.[2], William[1]) was born on 03 Mar 1891 in Caradoc township ON. He died on 27 Oct 1940 in ON. He married (1) MAY WALTERS in Sep 1921. She died on 03 May 1925. He married (2) MARGARET HENNERMAN on 15 Aug 1931.

Walter James Phillips and May Walters had the following child:

108   i.   ALICE MARGARET[4] PHILLIPS was born on 29 Jun 1992. She married John W. Wilkinson on 15 Apr 1942.

~~~~~~~~~~~~~~~~~~~~~~~~~~~~~~~

24.   JOHN GORDON[3] PHILLIPS (James F.[2], William[1]) was born on 22 Jan 1894 in Caradoc township ON. He died on 06 Jun 1939 in Caradoc township ON. He married JEAN MCKAY. She was born in 1898. She died on 13 Feb 1990 in Caradoc township ON.

John Gordon Phillips and Jean McKay had the following children:

109   i.   JAMES MURRAY*PHILLIPS was born on 24 Jan 1924. He died in 1944.

110   ii.   ROY MCKAY PHILLIPS was born on 31 May 1926.

111   iii.   JOHN WILFRED PHILLIPS was born on 15 Oct 1932. He married an unknown spouse on 05 Mar 1955 in St Thomas ON.

112   iv.   ROBERT GORDON PHILLIPS.

113   v.   WILLIAM ERNEST PHILLIPS.

25   RICHARD ROY^3 PHILLIPS (James F.^{2}, William^1) was born on 08 Jun 1896 in Caradoc township ON. He died on 17 Oct 1956 in Strathroy,ON. He married Gladys Beattie on 10 Feb 1920. She was born on 08 Jun 1897. She died on 05 Aug 1980 in Strathroy ON.

Richard Roy Phillips and Gladys Beattie had the following children:

114   i.   EDNA WINNIFRED*PHILLIPS was born on 05 May 1922.

115   ii.   ANNA MARIE ELIZABETH PHILLIPS born on 12 Nov 1935.

notes: Gen 3

Generation 4

61.   RICHARD BRUCE[4] PHILLIPS (William[3], Richard[2], William[1]) was born on 30 Sep 1884 in ON. He died in 1960. He married Gertrude Turner on 30 Oct 1917. She was born in 1883 in England and came to Canada by herself at age 10. (Perhaps as a Dr. Bernardo placement child). She died in 1917. Richard Bruce Phillips ran a grocery store on Thames St. Ingersoll where they lived over the store. Later he farmed at Folden's Lot 28 Blind Front Con. West Oxford. Her parents were Samuel Turner and Hannah Ward.

Richard Bruce Phillips and Gertrude Turner had the following child:
116   i. LLOYD RUSSELL[5] PHILLIPS. Lloyd Russell was born Nov 24, 1918. He married Margaret McKillen on 05 Sep 1953 at Weston ON. She was born Nov 7, 1925. They farmed on family farm lot 28, B.F. Con West Oxford. He also was a custodian at IDCI and she was a school teacher. They has a stillborn daughter Oct 18, 1955 who is buried with her father Bruce.

~~~~~~~~~~~~~~~~~~~~~~~~~~

62   GEORGE ROYAL[4] PHILLIPS (William[3], Richard[2], William[1]) was born in 1866 in ON. He died in 1957. He married MARY MARGARET BERDAN. She was born in 1887 in Bayham township. She died on 05 Mar 1933 in Oxford co ON.

George Royal Phillips and Mary Margaret Berdan had the following children:

117   i. ALLAN ROY[5] PHILLIPS was born in 1909. He died in 1993.
118   ii. HAZEL MARGARET PHILLIPS was born in 1911. She died in 1993.
119   iii. HARRY PHILLIPS was born in 1915. He died in 1977.

63   WALLACE ADAM^4 PHILLIPS (William^3, Richard^2, William^1) was born April 16 1895 in Oxford co ON. He died July 19, 1960 in Oxford co ON. He married CORRIE AURELIA KNEAL June 12, 1915. He was a grocer. She was born Jan 6 1898 in Woodstock. They lived at 340 Wellington St. Ingersoll. Her parents were Fred Kneal and Lillian Emigh.

Wallace Adam Phillips and Corrie Aurelia Kneal had the following child:

120   i.   DORA^5 (Doris) PHILLIPS.

65   ELIZABETH   LOUISE^4 PHILLIPS   (John   Martin^3,   Richard^2, William^1) was born on 20 Nov 1901 in Oxford co ON. She died in Nov 1987 in Orillia, Simcoe, ON, Canada. She married ROBERT PONTON. He was born on 02 Jun 1899 in Edinburgh Scotland. He died on 16 Nov 1968 in Newmarket ON. She may have been married to John Chisholm.

Robert Ponton and Elizabeth Louise Phillips had the following child:

121   i.   MARGARET ELIZABETH^5 PONTON was born on 18 Dec 1929 in Toronto ON. She died on 08 Apr 2008 in Orillia, Simcoe cty, ON. She married ??? CREW.

75   VELMA^4 ANNE HUGHES (Martha^3, Richard^2, William^1)born 1895. She married WILLIAM R. SAGE. He was born in 1894 in West Oxford ON. He died in 1942 in Ingersoll ON. Velma Hughes: second husband RALPH WILLIAMS 1888 -1960. Velma died at Ingersoll 1972.

William R. Sage and Velma Hughes had the following children:

122   i.   RONALD HUGHES[5] SAGE was born in 1917. He died in 1989. He married JEAN LUELLA BROWN. She was born in 1917. She died in 1998.

123   ii.   CHARLES EVERETT SAGE was born in 1921 in Beachville ON. He died in 1921 in Beachville ON.

124   iii.   WILLIAM ALLAN SAGE was born in 1922. He died in 2007. He married DOROTHY HENEY.

~~~~~~~~~~~~~~~~

82.   EDNA MAE[4] PHILLIPS (George[3], Richard[2], William[1]) was born in 1892 in Ingersoll ON. She died on 20 Jan 1923 in Oxford co ON. She married THOMAS WILLIAM PARKER. He was born on 21 Jan 1886 in East Zorra ON. He died on 05 Aug 1973 in Embro ON.

Thomas William Parker and Edna Mae Phillips had the following children:

125   i.   LAURETTA ABIGAIL[5] PARKER was born on 06 Oct 1911. She married Kenneth Edmund McIntyre on 05 July 1941 in Point Edward, Lambton cty, ON. He was born on 06 Sep 1909 in Point Edward, Lambton, cty, ON. He died on 06 May 1992.

126   ii.   JOHN WILFRED PARKER was born on 14 Dec 1913. He died on 15 Dec 1987 in Ingersoll ON. He married Edith Pauline McKee, daughter of William John McKee and Myrtle Annie Chew on 12 Mar 1938 in Embro ON. She was born on 14 Dec 1919 in York ON. She died in 1987 in London ON.

127   iii.   RUTH OLIVE PARKER was born on 23 Mar 1916 in West Zorra tp. Oxford cty. She married MICHAEL JOHN MINIHANE. He was born in Cork, Ireland. He died on 03 Mar 1993 in Tavistock, Oxford, ON.

128   iv. RALPH BUDD PARKER was born on 09 Dec 1917 in West Zorra tp. Oxford cty. He married Beatrice Arnetta Kugler on 07 Sep 1940 in Southampton, Bruce, ON. She was born on 04 Jul 1918 in Southampton, Bruce, ON. She died on 24 Jul 1992 in Ingersoll ON.

129   v. ALVIN ALLAN PARKER was born on 16 Jun 1920 in Embro ON West Zorra twp. He died on 01 Aug 1966 in Embro ON West Zorra twp. He married Florence June Noviss on 01 Jun 1946 in Woodstock ON. She was born on 19 Jun 1927 in Brantford ON.

vi.   BABY PARKER was born on 20 Jan 1923 in Oxford co ON. Baby died on 20 Jan 1923 in Oxford co ON.

Lorne Phillips, on left, mother Martha, wife Hilda, father George and neighbor lady, his four children spring 1943 at Paris.

84   ALBERT LORNE[4] PHILLIPS (George[3], Richard[2], William[1]) was born on 26 Apr 1905 in West Oxford twp Oxford county. He died July 18, 1967 in Brantford ON. He married Augusta Amanda Maria Rasmussen on 24 Dec 1931 in Woodstock ON. She was born in Oct 1906 and arrived in Canada Oct 3 1928 age 21. Lorne was a talented man who taught himself how to play the piano and other instruments. He worked as a weaver in Woodstock at La France textiles where he made the company samples. During the depression he built his own loom and made mats at home which he sold as a side business. Later he got a job in Brantford but as there were few houses available, they lived in Paris in an apartment over Ritt's Grill at 73 Dumfries St. He worked at Morso before working in the office at Massey, a job from which he retired. In Brantford they lived at 112 Grand River Ave. which was on the river and the house featured a player piano. His wife Hilda

worked at Barber Ellis, a paper company. Her mother Karen from Denmark lived with them. Karen was born Jan 5 1886 and died Aug 17 1961. Hilda was born in Odense Denmark to C. Lind and Karen. She had 3 Pederson half brothers and a half sister. Hilda first worked at Woodstock Rubber making rubber boots. She lost contact with her family until after WW2 when her mother came to NY where she and son George met her and brought her to Brantford. Consequently several trips were made to Denmark and Canada until 1956 when her mother remained in Canada until she died. Her missing arm was due to a train accident in Denmark.

Albert Lorne Phillips and Hilda Augusta Amanda Maria Rasmussen had the following children:

130   i.   RICHARDT DONALD LORNE[5] PHILLIPS was born on 22 Oct 1934 in Woodstock ON. He married Helen Elizabeth Bruce on 16 Jun 1962 in Ingersoll ON. She was born on 29 Jan 1940 in Ingersoll ON

131   ii. GEORGE CECIL PETER PHILLIPS was born on 29 Sep 1936 in Woodstock ON. He married Donna Walters on 20 Jun 1959 in Woodstock ON. She was born on 25 Sep 1939 in Blenheim Twp, Oxford Co ON.

132   iii. MYRNA MARGARET GAIL PHILLIPS was born on 17 Jan 1938 in Woodstock ON. She married James Fredrick Town on 07 Apr 1956 in Brantford ON. He was born on 18 Jan 1934 in Waterford, Haldimand, ON.

133   iv. ELWOOD STANLEY PHILLIPS was born on 24 Feb 1943 in Paris ON. He married Marie Eileen Rutherford in 1968. She was born on 16 Feb 1947 in Brantford ON.

Sandy, Dorothy and Gerry Sanders

86   DOROTHY MAE PHILLIPS (George[3], Richard[2], William[1]) was born on 01 May 1910 in Ingersoll ON Canada. She died on 31 Jan 1994 in Embro ON West Zorra twp. She married Alexander (Sandy) James Sanders on 11 Jul 1929 in Woodstock ON. He was born on 18 Oct 1909 in Embro ON West Zorra twp. He died on 13 Jul 1977 in Embro ON West Zorra twp. Dorothy Mae was the daughter of Myrtle Phillips 1889 but raised by grand parents George and Martha as their own. Don Philips was an adult when he learned she was not his older sister but his cousin. Her father is unknown. Dorothy and her husband had a bakery for 16 years at Rectory and Dundas in London ON. She was an active member of the Legion branch 317. Dorothy was raised as if she were generation four, but in reality she was generation 5. Therefore her lineage would make Gerald generation 6 and his children generation 7 and so forth.

        Alexander James Sanders and Dorothy Mae Phillips had the following child:

134   i. GERALD ALEXANDER SANDERS was born on 26 Feb 1936 in Woodstock ON. He married Madlyne Arlie Louise McLeod on 17 Aug 1955 in London ON. She was born on 28 Jan 1939 in London, ON. They divorced.

~~~~~~~~~~~~~~~~~~~~~~~~~~~~~~~~~~

Don Phillips and Margaret Martindale in 1930's

87.   DONALD TRUMAN[4] PHILLIPS (George[3], Richard[2], William[1]) was born on 24 Jan 1912 in Ingersoll ON Canada. He died on 25 Jun 1974 in Woodstock ON. He married Margaret Martindale on 05 Oct 1939 in Paris ON. She was born on 18 Jul 1910 in Darwin Lancashire England. She died on 04 Jan 1973 in Woodstock ON.

Don Phillips worked at Penmen's in Paris ON. His wife Margaret had worked there for sometime. While at Penman's Don became friends with Tony Gretsky who lived at Canning near Paris and had a market garden.

Walter Gretsky, Tony's son, was a good hockey player and played for the Paris junior C team where Don acted as trainer with the kids. Walter was the father of Wayne Gretsky one of the all time great hockey players. Don was a hunter, fisherman, hockey and baseball player and coached kids in sports. He was very gregarious and liked people. In later years he and Margaret were members of the NCHA, a camping group which they enjoyed. He moved to Woodstock from Paris in 1955 and got a position with a new start up in the city, Fisher Controls. He assembled valves on his own workbench. A smoker he became afflicted with lung issues and had a heart attack in his 50's. Don was one of the first to retire from the company. He was 62 when he died in 1974. Margaret began working at Penman's when she was 15 as did her brother Bill. Her mother also worked there. She bought herself a car and she and a friend briefly went to work in Hamilton at a clothing company there but returned to again work at Penman's who valued her work ethic. She quit after Brenda was born in 1941. Margaret died of an embolism 3 weeks after being hit by a truck while crossing Mill street on her way to work. The driver had not cleared the frost off his windshield. In Woodstock they rented a house at 282 Delatre Street and later an apartment on Main St.

Donald Truman Phillips and Margaret Martindale had the following children:

135   i.   BRENDA ELIZABETH PHILLIPS was born on 20 Oct 1941 in Paris ON. She married Sverre John Clausen on 24 Aug 1963 in Woodstock ON. He was born on 12 Jul 1941 in Toronto ON. He died on 26 Dec 2008 in Brantford ON.

136   ii.   DONNA MARGARET⁵ PHILLIPS was born on 07 May 1948 in Paris ON. She married John McBride Eacott on 20 Mar 1971 in Thamesford ON. He was born on 19 Jul 1937 in Timmins ON.

~~~~~~~~~~~~~~~~~~~~~~~~~~~~~~~~

81   MYRTLE JANE⁴ PHILLIPS (George³, Richard², William¹) was born on 15 Feb 1890 in Dereham twp Oxford county. She died on 29 Jan 1965 in Woodstock ON. She married Ernest Fredrick Scott on 23 Jul 1912 in Ingersoll. He was born in 1890 in Eaton Norfolk, England. He died in Sep 1958 in Woodstock ON. In 1914 he joined the army as part of the Oxford Rifles and then signed up with the 34ᵗʰ Battalion of the CEF in January 1915. He further signed up in February 1916 with the 168 overseas expeditionary force but the ship sailed without him as he was discharged as medically unfit due to anklyosis of the left shoulder, a debilitating injury in July 1916. The army record said he was 5ft 8 in tall, blonde, blue eyed, fair complexion and worked as a machine hand.

Ernest Fredrick Scott and Myrtle Jane Phillips had the following children:

137   ii. MARY ANN SCOTT was born on 08 Apr 1913 in Ingersoll She died in Dorchester ON. She married George Henry Skinner on 26 May 1933 in Ingersoll ON. He was born on 26 Mar 1910 in Mossley, Middlesex county. He died on 09 Jul 1967 in Dorchester ON.

138   iii. ELSIE LEONE SCOTT was born on 30 Jan 1916 in Woodstock ON. She died in Woodstock ON. She married Harry Walker on 21 Oct 1939 in Woodstock ON. He was born on 30 Nov 1913. He died on 01 Aug 1980 in Woodstock ON.

139   iv. MARTHA ELIZABETH SCOTT was born on 18 Jun 1918. She died on 16 Jan 1967 in Woodstock ON. She married ROBERT CYRIL MCGREGOR. She married CHARLES FRANCIS PATRICK TOOHEY. He was born on 14 Oct 1893 in Eastwood/Woodstock, ON. He died on 03 Apr 1967 in Woodstock ON

~~~~~~~~~~~~~~~~~~~~~~~~~~~~~

95   LILLIAN JEAN^4 PHILLIPS (William George^3, James F.^{2}, William^1) was born on 23 Apr 1916 in Caradoc township ON. She married Hugh Leslie Walker on 05 Jul 1941.

Hugh Leslie Walker and Lillian Jean Phillips had the following children:

141   i.   CAROLINE MARIE^5 WALKER was born on 23 Mar 1942. She married GARY PERLY.
142   ii.   SHARON JEAN WALKER was born on 29 Mar 1945. She married JOHN MARKLE.
143   iii. JANET LOUISE WALKER was born on 08 Jan 1950.

~~~~~~~~~~~~~~~~~~~~~~~~~~~~~

96   WALTER BLAIR^4 PHILLIPS (William George^3, James F.^{2}, William^1) was born on 06 May 1918 in Caradoc township ON. He died on 05 Jan 1989 in London ON. He married Margaret Joan Dagg on 15 Jul 1954 in London ON. She was born on 14 Oct 1922 in Kamsack, Saskatchewan. She died on 01 Aug 1989 in London ON.

Walter Blair Phillips and Margaret Joan Dagg had the following children:

144   i.   NANCY JEAN^5 PHILLIPS was born on 22 May 1955 in London ON. She married Frank Lucksi on 19 Dec 1981 in London ON.

145   ii.   GORDON WALTER PHILLIPS was born on 22 Nov 1956 in London ON. He married YVONNE UNKNOWN. She was born on 09 Jul 1983.

146   iii.   KATHRYN MARGARET PHILLIPS was born on 04 Feb 1958 in London ON.

147   iv.   STEVEN BLAIR PHILLIPS was born on 07 Mar 1960 in London ON. He married KATHY UNKNOWN.

148   v.   MICHAEL JAMES PHILLIPS was born on 11 Aug 1961 in London ON.

~~~~~~~~~~~~~~~~~~~~~~~~~~~~~

98   JAMES WILLIAM^4 REYNOLDS (Mary Elizabeth^3, James F.^{2}, William^1) was born on 16 Feb 1916 in Ailsa Craig, Middlesex cty,ON. He died on 18 Jul 1958 in London ON. He married Gwendolyn Ethel Ruth Mountenay on 21 Aug 1943 in Tillsonburg, ON. She was born on 13 Oct 1924 in Ommemee ON

James William Reynolds and Gwendolyn Ethel Ruth Mountenay had the following children:

150   i.   CAROL ANN^5 REYNOLDS was born on 30 May 1944 in London ON. She married WILLIAM RHODES. She married (2) DARCY TURNER DINGLE on 25 Jul 1992 in Toronto ON. He died 05/30/2019

151   ii.   WILLIAM JOSEPH REYNOLDS was born on 20 Jan 1948 in London ON. He married ROSE MARIE MCDONALD.

152   iii. JANICE ELIZABETH   REYNOLDS was born on 01 Dec 1952 in London ON.

153   iv. KAREN RUTH REYNOLDS was born on 28 Jun 1954 in London ON. She married FRED SCHAKEL

~~~~~~~~~~~~~~~~~~~~~~~~

99   JOHN HOWARD[4] REYNOLDS (Mary Elizabeth[3] Phillips, James F.[2] Phillips, William[1] Phillips) was born on 13 Nov 1917 in London ON. He married Nora Emily Harris on 29 Jun 1946 in London ON. She was born on 01 Nov 1922 in London ON.

John Howard Reynolds and Nora Emily Harris had the following children:

154   i. DONNA LOUISE[5] REYNOLDS was born on 07 May 1949 in Collingwood, ON. She married Allan Burnett Clemo on 03 Jun 1972 in London ON. He was born on 15 Sep 1939 in Stratford, ON.

155   ii. RICHARD DAVID REYNOLDS was born on 29 Sep 1952 in Peterborough, ON. He married Barbara Anne Black on 28 Sep 1978 in Calgary, Alberta. She was born on 08 Sep 1955 in Winnipeg, Manitoba.

156   iii. WARREN CRAIG REYNOLDS was born on 21 Nov 1957 in Peterborough, ON, Canada. He married Melinda Frances Rebecca Vemeth on 26 Jun 1982 in London ON. She was born on 24 Dec 1959 in London ON.

~~~~~~~~~~~~~~~~~~~~~~~~

100   GORDON ALFRED[4] REYNOLDS (Mary Elizabeth[3], James F.[2] William[1]) was born on 21 Apr 1920 in Hensall, Huron, ON, Canada. He married Alma Noreen Howe on 14 Aug 1948 in London ON. She was born on 22 Sep 1925 in London ON.

Gordon Alfred Reynolds and Alma Noreen Howe had the following child:

157   i.   JOHN ALLEN[5] REYNOLDS was born on 12 Dec 1948 in London ON

~~~~~~~~~~~~~~~~~~~~~~~~~~~~~~

101   CLIFFORD STANLEY[4] REYNOLDS (Mary Elizabeth[3], James F.[2], William[1]) was born on 18 Nov 1921 in London ON. He died on 18 Nov 1998 in London ON. He married Mary Isabelle Jacobs on 10 Feb 1945 in London ON. She was born on 21 Jul 1927.

       Clifford Stanley Reynolds and Mary Isabelle Jacobs had the following children:

158   i.   VERNON HOWARD[5] REYNOLDS was born on 31 Dec 1945 in London ON. He married DONNA ?   July 12, 1970

159   ii.   CLIFFORD JAMES REYNOLDS was born on 31 Dec 1946.

160   iii.   BRUCE RAYMOND REYNOLDS was born on 15 Mar 1948. He married NANCY GERTRUDE COLE, Aug 16, 1975. Nancy was born Nov 20 1951.

161   iv.   GLORIA JEAN REYNOLDS was born on 15 May 1949. She married unknown BAVERSTOCK.

162   v.   KENNETH EDWARD REYNOLDS (LEWIS) was born on 08 Jun 1953.

163`   vi.   PHILIP LOUIS REYNOLDS was born on 24 Jul 1954.

~~~~~~~~~~~~~~~~~~~~~~~~~~~~~~

104   VERNON CYRUS[4] REYNOLDS (Mary Elizabeth[3], James F.[2], William[1]) was born on 22 Mar 1926 in London ON. He married Helen Jean Walker on 10 Jun 1950 in London ON. She was born on 01 Jul 1927 in London ON.

Vernon Cyrus Reynolds and Helen Jean Walker had the following children:

164   i. KEITH WAYNE[5] REYNOLDS was born on 05 Apr 1953. He married Darlene Matthews on 30 Jul 1977. She was born in Port Burwell, ON. Keith died Jan 29, 1999.

165   ii. NANCY JEAN REYNOLDS was born on 28 Oct 1956 in Tillsonburg, ON.

166   iii. MARY HELEN REYNOLDS was born on 22 May 1960. She died on 16 Jan 1963 in London ON.

167   iv. MARLENE LYN REYNOLDS was born on 11 Jun 1965 in Tillsonburg, ON. She married Scott Bernard Lynds on 29 July 1989 in London ON.

~~~~~~~~~~~~~~~~~~~~~~~~~~~~~~~~~~

105   DONALD JAMES[4] BALLANTINE (Mabel Ellen[3], James F.[2], William[1]) was born on 15 Jun 1916 in Caradoc township ON. He died on 16 Aug 1985 in Mt Brydges,ON. He married Doris Cobban in 1947 in Caradoc township ON. She was born on 08 Oct 1920.

Donald James Ballantine and Doris Cobban had the following children:

168   i. ELIZABETH ANN[5] BALLANTINE was born on 12 Nov 1949 in London ON. She married UNKNOWN MARSHALL.

169   ii. LINDA CHRISTINE BALLANTINE was born on 19 July 1952. She married GORDON MURRAY.

170   iii. JANICE MARION BALLANTINE was born on 29 Mar 1955 in London ON. She married Edward Orr in Caradoc township ON. He

was born on 24 Jan 1955 in Caradoc township ON.

171   iv.   JAMES BALLANTINE was born on 19 Aug 1958.

106   DOROTHYISABEL^{4}BALLANTYNE(MabelEllen^3,JamesF.^{2},William^1) was born on 15 Jan 1922. She died on 07 Oct 1998 in Mt Brydges, ON. She married HARRY STINSON McCRAKEN. He was born in 1916.

Harry Stinson McCraken and Dorothy Isabel Ballantyne had the following children:

172   i. MARY ELIZABETH^5 McCRAKEN.

173   ii. NANCY ISABEL McCRAKEN was born on 15 Dec 1948 in London ON. She married JOHN LE FEUVRE.

174   iii. KATHERINE ANNE McCRAKEN was born on 27 Oct 1960.
She married GORDON MORRELL.

107 MARION   ELIZABETH^4 BALLANTINE (Mabel Ellen^3, James F.^{2}, William^1) was born on 16 Aug 1925. She married ROBERT STEEPE.

Robert Steepe and Marion Elizabeth Ballantine had the following children:

175 i.   ROBERT PAUL^5 STEEPE.

176 ii.   BARBARA JEAN STEEPE.

177 iii.   DAVID ANDREW STEEPE.

108   ALICE MARGARET^4 PHILLIPS (Walter James^3, James F.^{2}, William^1) was born on 29 June,(no year). She married John W. Wilkinson on 15 Apr 1942.

John W. Wilkinson and Alice Margaret Phillips had the following children:

178 i. PATRICIA^5 WILKINSON was born on 01 Apr 1943. She died in 1987. She married LARRY SHELDON.

179 ii. MAUREEN LISA WILKINSON. She married Brian Garner on 30 Jan 1961.

180 iii. JACQUELINE WILKINSON was born on 22 Aug1949. She married James August Spagnolo on 21 Sep 1968.

~~~~~~~~~~~~~~~~~~~~~~~~~~~

111. JOHN WILFRED^4 PHILLIPS (John Gordon^3, James F.^{2}, William^1) was born on15 Oct 1932. He married an unknown spouse on 05 Mar 1955 in St Thomas ON.

John Wilfred Phillips had the following children:

181 i. BRIAN MURRAY^5 PHILLIPS was born on 27 Aug 1956

182 ii. BARRY GORDON PHILLIPS was born on 15 Dec 1958. He married Lisa Kay on 14 May 1988 in London ON.

183 iii. ROBERT GORDON PHILLIPS.

184 iv. WILLIAM ERNEST PHILLIPS.

Generation 5

116_LLOYD_RUSSELL[5]PHILLIPS(RichardBruce[4],William[3],Richard[2],William[1]). Lloyd Russell married Margaret McKillen on 05 Sep 1953.

Lloyd Russell Phillips and Margaret McKillen had the following child:

185   i.   KAREN RUTH[6] PHILLIPS was born on 18 Oct 1955.

120   DORIS PHILLIPS (Wallace [4], William, Richard, William) born Jan 10, 1920, married Sep 25, 1940. Richard Seldon who was born Aug 6, 1915 to Arthur Seldon and Clara Edith Dundas.

      Doris and Richard had the following children:

317 i JANET ELAINE SELDON born Aug 24 1944 married May 30, 1970 to Clive Tompkins born May4, 1942.

318   ii RUTH ELIZABETH SELDON born April 10 1946, married (1) Jack Laverne Hutson June 5, 1965 married (2) Bruce Wayne Flood Dec 15, 1978.

319   iii LINDA MARIANNE SELDON born 11 Dec 1950, married Aug 1 1970 to Gary John McLay born April 14 1951 live at 126 Innes St. Ingersoll.

320   iv ROBERT GEORGE SELDON born Jan 11, 1953 married Susan Kathleen Kimberley born May 7 1952. They Farmed at RR 3 Ingersoll.

129   ALVIN[5] PARKER (Edna Mae[4], George[3], Richard[2], William[1]). Alvin died on 03 Aug 1966 in Beachville ON.

Alvin Parker had the following child:

186   i.   PATRICIA GAIL[6] PARKER was born in 1946 in Ingersoll ON. She died in 1949 in Ingersoll ON.

~~~~~~~~~~~~~~~~~~~~~~~~~~~~~

126.   JOHN WILFRED[5] PARKER (Edna Mae[4], George[3], Richard[2], William[1])was born on 14 Dec 1913. He died on 15 Dec 1987 in Ingersoll ON. He married Edith Pauline McKee, daughter of William John McKee and Myrtle Annie Chew on 12 Mar 1938 in Embro ON. She was born on 14 Dec 1919 in York ON. She died in 1987 in London ON.

John Wilfred Parker and Edith Pauline McKee had the following children:

187   i.   JANICE LYNN[6] PARKER. She married Douglas Murray Wallace on 27 Aug 1977 in Toronto ON.

188   ii.   WILLIAM ALAN PARKER was born on 11 Apr 1938. He married EVE UNKNOWN.

189   iii.   BRUCE DONALD PARKER was born on 16 Jul 1940 in North Bay, Nipissing, ON. He married BETTY JANE UNKNOWN. She was born in North Bay, Nipissing, ON.

~~~~~~~~~~~~~~~~~~~~~~~~~~~~~

130. RICHARDT DONALD LORNE[5] PHILLIPS (Albert Lorne[4], George[3], Richard[2], William[1]) was born on 22 Oct 1934 in Woodstock ON. He married Helen Elizabeth Bruce on 16 Jun 1962 in Ingersoll ON. She was born on 29 January 1940 in Ingersoll ON.

Richardt, who took shop in high school, got a job at 18 fixing sewing machines at Watson in Brantford. He next did a fill in repair work at Penman's in Paris that turned into working for 15years before business slowed. He eventually left to work at Fisher Controls in Woodstock at the urging of his uncle Don. Richardt retired from Fisher having been a lathe operator and later worked in supervision. Richardt was a skilled woodworker and represented manufacturers at wood shows in retirement. Richardt lived on Victoria Street in Woodstock for many years.

Richardt Donald Lorne Phillips and Helen Elizabeth Bruce had the following children:

190   i. STEPHEN RICHARD[6] PHILLIPS was born on 24 Apr 1963 in Woodstock ON. He married Darlene Pandora Wilson on 24 September 1988 in Woodstock ON.

191   ii. DAVID EDWARD PHILLIPS was born on 18 Aug 1965 in Woodstock ON.

~~~~~~~~~~~~~~~~~~~~~~~~~~~~~~~~

131.   GEORGE CECIL PETER[5] PHILLIPS (Albert Lorne[4], George[3], Richard[2], William[1]) was born on 29 Sep 1936 in Woodstock ON. He married Donna Walters on 20 Jun 1959 in Woodstock ON. She was born on 25 Sep 1939 in Blenheim Twp, Oxford Co

233.   George Cecil Peter Phillips and Donna Walters had the following children:

234   i. SUSAN LYNN[6] PHILLIPS was born on 17 May 1960 in Brantford ON. She married Terrance Gambacourt on 17 Jul 1982 in Brantford ON

235   ii.   GREGORY GEORGE PHILLIPS was born on 24 May 1963.

236   iii.   DIANE ELIZABETH PHILLIPS was born on 15 Jan 1966 in Brantford ON.

~~~~~~~~~~~~~~~~~~~~~~~~~~~~~~

132   MYRNA MARGARET GAIL[5] PHILLIPS (Albert Lorne[4],

George[3], Richard[2], William[1]) was born on 17 Jan 1938 in Woodstock ON She married James Fredrick Town on 07 Apr 1956 in Brantford ON. He was born on 18 Jan 1934 in Waterford, Haldimand, ON, .

James Fredrick Town and Myrna Margaret Gail Phillips had the following children:

237   i. JAMES ALBERT FREDRICK[6] TOWN was born on 22 Nov 1957. He married Gloria Ann Raycroft on 06 Aug 1977 in Paris ON. She was born on 05 Jun 1959 in Paris ON.

238   ii. SHARON ELLEN MARIE TOWN was born on 15 Dec 1958 in Paris ON.

239   iii. CATHERINE LEE ANN TOWN was born on 09 Nov 1962 in Paris ON. She married Robert James Coombs on 22 Aug 1983 in Paris ON. He was born on 12 Dec 1962.

240   iv. LAURA LYNN TOWN was born on 18 Jun 1964 in Paris ON. She married David Wayne Peart on 23 Jul 1983 in Paris ON. He was born on 21 Oct 1961.

133   ELWOOD STANLEY[5] PHILLIPS (Albert Lorne[4], George[3], Richard[2], William[1]) was born on 24 Feb 1943 in Paris ON. He married Marie Eileen Rutherford in 1968. She was born on 16 Feb 1947 in Brantford ON.

Elwood Stanley Phillips and Marie Eileen Rutherford had the following child:

241   i. WARREN JAMES[6] PHILLIPS was born on 02 Aug 1969.

134   GERALD ALEXANDER SANDERS (Dorothy Mae Phillips, George[3] Phillips, Richard[2] Phillips, William[1] Phillips) was born on 26 Feb 1936 in

Woodstock ON. He married Madlyne Arlie Louise McLeod on 17 Aug 1955 in London ON. She was born on 28 Jan 1939 in London, ON. She died. For 30 years Gerry owned and operated Sanders On The Beach, a popular bar restaurant on the beach at Grand Bend . The Kennedy family cottage at Grand Bend became an indoor dining place in 1953 until 1973 when Jerry bought it. His partner Ed was hired to work there. In 1980 the establishment was the first in Ontario to have a patio liquor licence. They expanded to have seating for over 600 inside and out. Gerry married Edward Arnett Oct 20 2005 . Edward died 9 February, 2021.

Gerald Alexander Sanders and Madlyne Arlie Louise McLeod had the following children:

192   i. KIMBERLEY ANNE SANDERS was born on 11 Feb 1956 in Exeter ON. She married Robert Donald Case on 2 Nov 1979 in London ON. He was born on 06 Oct 1954 in Exeter, ON. They owned a plumbing and electrical business in Grand Bend.

193   ii. ARLIE LOUISE SANDERS was born on 08 Feb 1958 in London ON. She married Craig David Saunders on 27 Feb 1988 in Grand Bend. She died 17 May 2015.He was born 11 October 1965 in Toronto and died 28 January 2011.

194   iii. GERALD ALEXANDER SANDERS was born on 19 May 1959 in London ON. He married Debra Anne Wydareny on 25 Jul 1981 in London ON. She was born on 29 Jul 1961 in London ON. They divorced. Gerald married Cheryl Ann Dunham on 22 Feb. 1997 in Scarborough ON.

~~~~~~~~~~~~~~~~~~~~~~~~~~~~

135   BRENDA ELIZABETH[5] PHILLIPS (Donald Truman[4], George[3],

Richard[2], William[1]) was born on 20 Oct 1941 in Paris ON. She married Sverre John Clausen on 24 Aug 1963 in Woodstock ON. He was born on 12 Jul 1941 in Toronto ON . He died on 26 Dec 2008 in Brantford ON.

Notes for Sverre John Clausen:

John was of Norwegian ancestry. John was raised by his adoptive mother and his adoptive father Sverre, also Norwegian who died when John was 4. John was raised in Kitchener ON by his mother Luella Clausen who was a nurse. John's sister Sally married Doug Bradley.

His biological father Rein Riber was an airman stationed in Canada who later became a doctor but suffered from a crippling disease. He married in Norway but had no other natural children. John's biological mother Eileen Walker married and moved to USA. She had a son Michael Spall of NYC and daughter Kathy Feinman of Lynchburg VA. Both have children. Late in his life John learned about his biological mother and half brother and half sister.

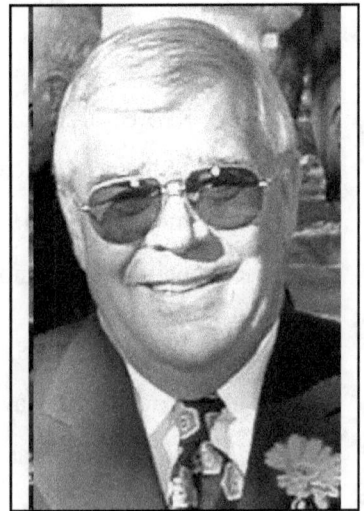

John was a computer salesman in the early days of large systems for business. He lived in Kitchener, Toronto, Edmonton and Brantford.

Sverre John Clausen and Brenda Elizabeth Phillips had the following children:

195   i.   KAREN LESLIE[6] CLAUSEN was born on 22 Dec 1964 in

Kitchener ON. She married Todd Yates on 13 Jun 1992 in Brantford ON. He was born in July 1964 in Toronto ON.

196 ii. KELLY ELIZABETH CLAUSEN was born on 22 Dec 1964 in Kitchener ON. She married Paul Andrew Callahan, son of Phyliss and Bud Callahan, on 30 June 1990 in Brantford ON. He was born on 09 Nov 1962 in London ON.

197 iii. SCOTT JEREMY CLAUSEN was born on 21 Dec 1975 in Mississauga ON. He married JENNY TREMBLAY 11 Oct 2003 at Apps Mill, Paris ON. She was born in Sep 1976 in Sudbury ON.

136 DONNA MARGARET^5 PHILLIPS (Donald Truman^4, George^3, Richard^2, William^1) was born on 07 May 1948 in Paris ON. She married John McBride Eacott, a master at Toronto Teachers' College, at 3 pm 20 Mar 1971 in Westminster United Church Thamesford ON. He was born on 19 July 1937 in Timmins ON.

John McBride Eacott and Donna Margaret Phillips had the following children:

198 i. ERIN LEE^6 EACOTT was born on 19 Apr 1974 in Toronto ON. She married Jason Unger on 23 Jun 2007 at Eacott residence, Curries ON. He was born on 18 Aug 1971 in Winnipeg, Manitoba.

199 ii. JONATHAN PHILLIPS EACOTT was born on 29 Apr 1977 in Woodstock ON. He married Amy Leigh Straus on 02 Aug 2008 in Michigan, USA. She was born on 04 Jan 1977 in Stratford, ON.

137   MARY ANN^5 SCOTT (Myrtle Jane^4, George^3, Richard^2, William^1) was born on 08 Apr 1913 in Ingersoll ON . She died in Dorchester ON. She married George Henry Skinner on 26 May 1933 in Ingersoll ON . He was born on 26 Mar 1910 in Mossley, Middlesex county. He died on 09 Jul 1967 in Dorchester ON.

George Henry Skinner and Mary Ann Scott had the following children:

200   i.   DOROTHY LOUISE^6 SKINNER.
201   ii.   MARY ELLEN SKINNER.
202   iii. DANIEL GEORGE SKINNER.
203   iv.   AMELIA ANN SKINNER.

138   ELSIE LEONE^5 SCOTT (Myrtle Jane^4, George^3, Richard^2, William^1 Phillips) was born on 30 Jan 1916 in Woodstock ON. She died in Woodstock ON. She married Harry Walker on 21 Oct 1939 in Woodstock ON. He was born on 30 Nov 1913. He died on 01 Aug 1980 in Woodstock ON.

Harry Walker and Elsie Leone Scott had the following children:

204   i. MARY JANE^6 WALKER was born on 17 Feb 1937 in Woodstock ON. She married BARNEY CARN/ KARN. He was born in Port Credit, Peel, ON.

205   ii. MICHAEL HARRY WALKER was born on 11 Jan 1942 in Glace Bay, Cape Breton, Nova Scotia, . He married HEATHER BOOMER. He married IRENE McISAAC.

206   iii. MARK IAN WALKER was born on 17 Jul 1956 in Woodstock O. He married CATHERINE ALLES.

139   MARTHA ELIZABETH[5] SCOTT (Myrtle Jane[4], George[3], Richard[2], William[1]) was born on 18 Jun 1918. She died on 16 Jan 1967 in Woodstock ON. She married ROBERT CYRIL MCGREGOR. She married CHARLES FRANCIS PATRICK TOOHEY. He was born on 14 Oct 1893 in Eastwood/Woodstock, ON. He died on 03 Apr 1967 in Woodstock ON.

Martha Elizabeth Scott and Robert Cyril McGregor had the following children:

207   i. ROBERT FREDERICK[6] MCGREGOR was born on 04 Oct 1936. He married Dorothy Joan Toohey on 20 Apr 1957 in Woodstock ON. She was born on 09 Aug 1939 in Woodstock ON.

208   ii. JAMES ALLAN McGREGOR was born on 09 Jun 1937 in Woodstock ON. He married Gabriel Lesley Knight on 07 Jun 1958 in Woodstock ON. She was born on 06 Jun 1942 in London, ON, .

209   iii. BON NIE ELIZABETH McGREGOR was born on 13 Dec 1941 in Woodstock ON. She married (1) GARY RICHARD GEILING on 11 Jun 1958 in Woodstock ON. She married (2) JOHN FREDERICK WILFORD on 09 Feb 1971 in Woodstock ON. He was born on 29 Jan 1934. He died on 08 Oct 1989 in Woodstock ON.

210.   iv. MARLENE ANN McGREGOR was born on 20 Jul 1943 in Woodstock ON. She married John William McClellan on 26 Feb 1965 in Woodstock ON
. He was born on 12 Jun 1933.

Second Marriage :**Martha Elizabeth Scott and** Charles Francis Patrick Toohey and had the following children:

211   v. VIRGINIA JOYCE[6] TOOHEY was born on 08 May 1948 in Woodstock ON. She married JAMES WILLIAM BRIAN KENNEDY in Jan 1967 . He was born on 30 Dec 1942 in Bracebridge ON. He died Oct 3, 2013 at Bracebridge ON

212   ii. TIMOTHY LEWIS TOOHEY was born on 09 Jan 1951 in Woodstock ON. He married Sandra May Foster on 22 Oct 1977 in Woodstock ON. She was born in Hamilton ON.

~~~~~~~~~~~~~~~~~~~~~~

125   LAURETTA ABIGAIL[5] PARKER (Edna Mae[4], George[3], Richard[2], William[1]) was born on 06 Oct 1911. She married Kenneth Edmund McIntyre on 05 Jul 1941 in Point Edward, Lambton, ON, . He was born on 06 Sep 1909 in Point Edward, Lambton, ON, . He died on 06 May 1992.

Kenneth Edmund McIntyre and Lauretta Abigail Parker had the following children:

213   i. KENNETH JAMES[6] MCINTYRE was born on 20 Oct 1944 in Port Huron, St Clair, Michigan, USA. He married Anita Grace Jordon on 11 Oct 1969 in St Clair, Michigan, USA. She was born on 29 Jan 1946 in Louisville, Jefferson, Kentucky, USA.

214   ii. PAUL DAVID MCINTYRE was born on 03 Jun 1946 in Port Huron, St Clair, Michigan, USA. He married Maureen Ellen Russell on 14 Oct 1978 in Flint, Genesee, Michigan, USA. She was born on 20 Jul 1958 in Flint, Genesee, Michigan, USA.

~~~~~~~~~~~~~~~~~~~~~~

127   RUTH OLIVE[5] PARKER (Edna Mae[4], George[3], Richard[2], William[1] Phillips) was born on 23 Mar 1916 in West Zorra tp. Oxford cty. She married MICHAEL JOHN MINIHANE. He was born in Cork, Ireland. He died on 03 Mar 1993 in Tavistock, Oxford, ON, .

Michael John Minihane and Ruth Olive Parker had the following children:

215   i.   PATRICK[6] MINIHANE.
216   ii.   MARY MINIHANE.
217   iii. ANNE MINIHANE.
218   iv.   JAMES MINIHANE.
219   v.   THOMAS MINIHANE.
220   vi.   MICHAEL MINIHANE.
221   vii. WILLIAM MINIHANE.

~~~~~~~~~~~~~~~~~~~~~~~~~~~~~~~~

128   RALPH BUDD[5] PARKER (Edna Mae[4], George[3], Richard[2], William[1] Phillips) was born on 09 Dec 1917 in West Zorra tp. Oxford cty. He married Beatrice Arnetta Kugler on 07 Sep 1940 in Southampton, Bruce, ON, . She was born on 04 Jul 1918 in Southampton, Bruce, ON, . She died on 24 Jul 1992 in Ingersoll ON .

Ralph Budd Parker and Beatrice Arnetta Kugler had the following children:

222   i   THOMAS RALPH[6] PARKER was born on 08 Aug 1941 in Ingersoll ON . He married Ruth Anne Wailes on 09 Nov 1963 in Ingersoll ON . She was born on 24 Nov 1944 in London ON.

223   ii.   LOIS HELEN PARKER was born on 29 Dec 1942 in Ingersoll ON . She married (1) GORDON EDWARD HUFFNAGEL on 27 Dec 1969 in Toronto ON . She married (2) ALAN WILSON in Apr 1980 in Toronto ON .

224   iii. PATRICIA ANNE PARKER was born on 20 Jan 1952.

225   iv. VIRGINIA GAYLE PARKER was born on 20 May 1954. She married SANDY BARTER.

~~~~~~~~~~~~~~~~~~~~~~~~~~

129   ALVIN ALLAN^5 PARKER (Edna Mae^4, George^3, Richard^2, William^1 Phillips) was born on 16 Jun 1920 in Embro ON West Zorra twp. He died on 01 Aug 1966 in Embro ON West Zorra twp. He married Florence June Noviss on 01 Jun 1946 in Woodstock ON. She was born on 19 Jun 1927 in Brantford ON.

Alvin Allan Parker and Florence June Noviss had the following children:

226   i. DANIEL ALLEN^6 PARKER.

227   ii. WANDA MAE PARKER.

228   iii. CHERYL MARIE PARKER was born on 17 Apr 1949.

229   iv. DEBORAH JUNE PARKER was born on 20 Feb 1951.

230   v. JACK LYNN PARKER was born on 26 Jul 1956.

231   vi. RICHARD WAYNE PARKER was born on 10 Apr 1958.

232   vii. CALVIN GEORGE PARKER was born on 01 Apr 1960.

~~~~~~~~~~~~~~~~~~~~~~~~~~

141   CAROLINE MARIE^5 WALKER (Lillian Jean^4, William George^3, James F.^{2}, William^1) was born on 23 Mar 1942. She married GARY PERLY

Gary Perly and Caroline Marie Walker had the following child:

242   i.   JAMES AMOS[6] PERLY.

~~~~~~~~~~~~~~~~~~~~~~~~~~~~~~

150   CAROL ANN[5] REYNOLDS (James William[4], Mary Elizabeth[3], James F.[2], William[1]) was born on 30 May 1944 in London ON. She married WILLIAM RHODES. She married (2) DARCY TURNER DINGLE on 25 July 1992 in Toronto ON .

William Rhodes and Carol Ann Reynolds had the following child:

243   i.   JAMES WILLIAM EUGENE[6] RHODES was born 28 Nov 1960.

~~~~~~~~~~~~~~~~~~~~~~~~~~~~~~

153   KAREN RUTH[5] REYNOLDS (James William[4], Mary Elizabeth[3], James F.[2], William[1]) was born on 28 Jun 1954 in London ON. She married FRED SCHAKEL.

Fred Schakel and Karen Ruth Reynolds had the following child:

244   i.   KEVIN REYNOLDS[6] SCHAKEL was born on 25 Aug 1995.

328   ii   IAN SCHAKEL born April 20, 1999

~~~~~~~~~~~~~~~~~~~~~~~~~~~~~~

154.   DONNA LOUISE[5] REYNOLDS (John Howard[4], Mary Elizabeth[3], James F.[2], William[1]) was born on 07 May 1949 in Collingwood, Simcoe, ON, . She married Allan Burnett Clemo on 03 Jun 1972 in London ON. He was born on 15 Sep 1939 in Stratford, ON.

Allan Burnett Clemo and Donna Louise Reynolds had the following child:

245   i.   LAURA   KATHLEEN^6 CLEMO was born on 11 May 1974 in London ON.

~~~~~~~~~~~~~~~~~~~~~~~~~~~~~

155   RICHARD DAVID^5 REYNOLDS (John Howard^4, Mary Elizabeth^3, James F.^{2}, William^1) was born on 29 Sep 1952 in Peterborough, ON, . He married Barbara Anne Black on 28 Sep 1978 in Calgary, Alberta, . She was born on 08 Sep 1955 in Winnipeg, Manitoba, .

Richard David Reynolds and Barbara Anne Black had the following children:

246   i.   JENNIFER LYNN^6 REYNOLDS was born on 22 Oct 1978 in Calgary, Alberta.

247   ii. CHRISTOPHER MARK REYNOLDS was born on 13 May 1981 in Windsor ON .

~~~~~~~~~~~~~~~~~~~~~~~~~~~~~

156   WARREN CRAIG^5 REYNOLDS (John Howard^4, Mary Elizabeth^3, James F.^{2}, William^1) was born on 21 Nov 1957 in Peterborough, ON, . He married Melinda Frances Rebecca Vemeth on 26 Jun 1982 in London ON. She was born on 24 Dec 1959 in London ON.

Warren Craig Reynolds and Melinda Frances Rebecca Vemeth had the following children:

248   i.   MICHELLE DENISE^6 REYNOLDS was born on 07 Feb 1986 in Leamington, Essex, ON, .

249   ii. DANIEL JAMES REYNOLDS was born on 15 Sep 1988 in Kitchener ON

250   iii. BRIAN ALEXANDER REYNOLDS was born on 10 Sep 1992 in Kitchener ON

~~~~~~~~~~~~~~~~~~~~~~~~~~~

158   VERNON HOWARD[5] REYNOLDS (Clifford Stanley[4], Mary Elizabeth[3], James F.[2], William[1]) was born on 31 Dec 1945 in London ON. He married DONNA unknown.

Vernon Howard Reynolds and Donna unknown had the following children:

251   i. KIMBERLEY ANN[6] REYNOLDS was born on 29 Jul 1972.

252   ii. MICHAEL SCOTT REYNOLDS was born on 08 Oct 1980.

~~~~~~~~~~~~~~~~~~~~~~~~~~~

160.   BRUCE RAYMOND[5] REYNOLDS (Clifford Stanley[4], Mary Elizabeth[3], James F.[2], William[1]) was born on 15 Mar 1948. He married NANCY unkown.

        Bruce Raymond Reynolds and Nancy unknown had the following children:

253   i. DAVID BRUCE[6] REYNOLDS was born on 30 Sep 1982.

~~~~~~~~~~~~~~~~~~~~~~~~~~~

162   KENNETH WAYNE[5] REYNOLDS (Vernon Cyrus[4], Mary Elizabeth[3], James F.[2], William[1]) was born on 05 Apr 1953. He married Darlene Matthews on 30 Jul 1977. She was born in Port Burwell, Elgin, ON, .

        Kenneth Wayne Reynolds and Darlene Matthews had the following children:

255   i.   ALLISON CHRISTIE^6 REYNOLDS was born on 28 Oct 1983. Tillsonburg

254   ii.   LEE -ANN ERIN REYNOLDS was born on 19 Jun 1981. Tillsonburg

168   ELIZABETH ANN^5 BALLANTINE (Donald James^4, Mabel Ellen^3, James F.^{2}, William^1) was born on 12 Nov 1949 in London ON. She married unknown MARSHALL.

    Marshall and Elizabeth Ann Ballantine had the following children:

256   i.   JANE ELIZABETH^6 MARSHALL was born on 17 Mar 1977.

257   ii.   SARA ANNE MARSHALL was born on 23 Jul 1979.

169   LINDA CHRISTINE^5 BALLANTINE (Donald James^4, Mabel Ellen^3, James F.^{2}, William^1) was born on 19 Jul 1952. She married GORDON MURRAY.

    Gordon Murray and Linda Christine Ballantine had the following child:

258   i.   KEVIN EDWARD^6 MURRAY was born on 23 Dec 1989.

170   JANICE MARION^5 BALLANTINE (Donald James^4, Mabel Ellen^3, James F.^{2}, William^1) was born on 29 Mar 1955 in London ON. He married Edward Orr in Caradoc township ON. He was born on 24 Jan 1955 in Caradoc township ON.

    Janice Marion Ballantine and Edward Orr had the following child:

259   i.   KATHERINE^6 ORR was born on 24 Apr 1983.

178 PATRICIA^5 WILKINSON (Alice Margaret^4, Walter James^3, James F.^{2}, William^1) was born on 01 Apr 1943. She died in 1987. She married LARRY SHELDON.

Larry Sheldon and Patricia Wilkinson had the following children:

260 i. KIRK^6 SHELDON.

261 ii. LISA SHELDON.

262 iii. JOHN SHELDON.

263 iv. BRAD SHELDON.

180 JACQUELINE^5 WILKINSON (Alice Margaret^4, Walter James^3, James F.^{2}, William^1) was born on 22 Aug 1949. She married James August Spagnolo on 21 Sep 1968.

James August Spagnolo and Jacqueline Wilkinson had the following child:

264 i. DINA MARIE^6 SPAGNOLO was born in 1970. She married JASON WELLS

Generation 6

188   WILLIAM ALAN^6 PARKER (John Wilfred^5, Edna Mae^4, George^3, Richard^2, William^1) was born on 11 Apr 1938. He married EVE unknown.

William Alan Parker and Eve unknown had the following child:

265   i. LINDA PAULINE ROSE^7 PARKER.

~~~~~~~~~~~~~~~~~~~~~~~~~~~~~~

189   BRUCE DONALD^6 PARKER (John Wilfred^5, Edna Mae^4, George^3, Richard^2, William^1) was born on 16 Jul 1940 in North Bay, Nipissing, ON, . He married BETTY JANE UNKNOWN. She was born in North Bay, Nipissing, ON, .

Bruce Donald Parker and Betty Jane unknown had the following children:

266   i. LAURIE^7 PARKER.

267   ii. MICHAEL JOHN PARKER.

~~~~~~~~~~~~~~~~~~~~~~~~~~~~~~

192   KIMBERLEY ANNE SANDERS (Gerald Alexander, Dorothy Mae, George^3, Richard^2, William^1) was born on 11 Feb 1956 in London ON. She married Robert Donald Case on 2 Aug 1979 in Exeter ON. He was born on 06 Oct 1954 in Exeter,ON.

Robert Donald Case and Kimberley Anne Sanders had the following children:

268   i. MIRANDA MAE CASE was born on 23 Sep 1982.

269   ii. STACY ELIZABETH CASE was born 24 July 1984. She died 4 June 2001.

270   iii. DAWN ARLIE CASE was born on 19 Apr 1987.

~~~~~~~~~~~~~~~~~~~~~~~~~~~~~~~

193   ARLIE LOUISE SANDERS (Gerald Alexander, Dorothy Mae George[3], Richard[2], William[1]) was born 8 Feb,1958 in London, on. She married Craig David Saunders on 27 Feb 1988 in Grand Bend.

She died 17 May 2015. Craig was born 11 Oct 1965 in Toronto. He died 28 January 2011.

Craig David Saunders and Arlie Louise Sanders had the following children:

331   i. Craig Alexander Saunders was born 26 July 1990

332   ii. Jack Stuart Saunders was born 27 Feb. 1994

194   GERALD ALEXANDER SANDERS (Gerald Alexander, Dorothy Mae, George[3], Richard[2], William[1]) was born on 10 May 1959 in London ON. He married Debra Anne Wydareny on 25 Jul 1981 in London ON. She was born on 29 Jul 1961 in London ON. They divorced. He married Cheryl Ann Dunham on 22 Feb 1997. She was born 12 May 1967 in Toronto.

Gerald Alexander Sanders and Debra Anne Wydareny had the following children:

271   i.   HALIE AMBER SANDERS was born on 13 Sep 1986.

329   ii.   SHELBY MORGAN SANDERS was born April 25 1989.

Gerald Alexander Sanders and Cheryl Ann Dunham had the following child:

330   i.   MADISON ALEXIS SANDERS was born 18 Jan 1996.
        Cheryl Dunham had two previous children.

331   i.   CHRISTOPHER MICHAEL DOUCETTE born 28 Sept 1985

332   ii.   NICOL RENEE DOUCETTE born 13 Feb 1989

195   KAREN LESLIE[6] CLAUSEN (Brenda Elizabeth[5], Donald Truman[4], George[3], Richard[2], William[1]) was born on 22 Dec 1964 in Kitchener ON . She married Todd Yates on 13 Jun 1992 in Brantford ON. He was born in Jul 1964 in Toronto ON .

Todd Yates and Karen Leslie Clausen had the following children:

272   i.   RYAN THOMAS[7] YATES was born on 05 Nov 1998 in Toronto

273   ii.   ADAM PHILLIP YATES was born on 05 Sep 2002 in Toronto

196.   KELLY ELIZABETH[6] CLAUSENwas born on 22 Dec 1964 in Kitchener ON. She married Paul Andrew Callahan, son of Bud Callahan and Phyliss on 30 Jun 1990 in Brantford ON. He was born on 09 Nov 1962 in London ON.

Paul Andrew Callahan and Kelly Elizabeth Clausen had the following children:

274   i.   SARAH ELIZABETH[7] CALLAHAN was born on 28 Jul 1992.

275   ii.   TYLER DOUGLAS CALLAHAN was born on 20 Apr 1994

197   SCOTT JEREMY CLAUSEN (Brenda Elizabeth[5], Donald Truman[4], George[3], Richard[2], William[1]) was born Dec 21, 1975. He married Jenny Elaine Tremblay at Apps Mill, Paris ON on Oct 11, 2003. She was daughter of Denise Benoit and G. Tremblay and she was born Sept 29, 1976

Scott and Jenny had the following child:

276   i   ELISSA ANN CLAUSEN was born June 11, 2015

~~~~~~~~~~~~~~~~~~~~~~~~~~~

198   ERIN LEE[6] EACOTT (Donna Margaret[5], Donald Truman[4], George[3], Richard[2] P, William[1]) was born on 19 Apr 1974 in Toronto ON . She married Jason Unger on 23 Jun 2007 at Eacott residence, Curries ON. He was born on 18 Aug 1971 in Winnipeg, Manitoba. Son of Brenda and Robert Unger.

Jason Unger and Erin Lee Eacott had the following children:

277   i.   AVEN WYNNE[7] UNGER was born on 07 June 2009 in Edmonton AB

278   ii.   TESSA NELL EACOTT was born on 13 Sep 2012 in Edmonton AB.

~~~~~~~~~~~~~~~~~~~~~~~~~~~

199   JONATHAN PHILLIPS[6] EACOTT (Donna Margaret[5], Donald Truman[4] , George[3], Richard[2], William[1]) was born on 29 Apr 1977 in Woodstock ON. He married Amy Leigh Straus.

Jonathan Phillips Eacott and Amy Leigh Straus had the following children:

279   i.   NATHAN STRAUS[7] EACOTT was born on 08 Jul 2014 in Riverside, California, USA.

280   ii.   MACKENZIE SUZANNE EACOTT was born on 08 Jul 2014 in Riverside, California, USA

~~~~~~~~~~~~~~~~~~~~~~~~~~~

204   MARY JANE[6] WALKER (Elsie Leone[5] Scott, Myrtle Jane[4], George[3], Richard[2], William[1]) was born on 17 Feb 1937 in Woodstock ON. She married BARNEY KARN. He was born in Port Credit, Peel, ON.

Barney Karn and Mary Jane Walker had the following children:

281   i.   BRIAN^7 KARN.

282   ii.   JOANNE KARN.

283   iii.   INFANT KARN.

~~~~~~~~~~~~~~~~~~~~~~~~~~~~

205   MICHAEL HARRY^6 WALKER (Elsie Leone^5 Scott, Myrtle Jane^4, George^3, Richard^2, William^1) was born on 11 Jan 1942 in Glace Bay, Cape Breton, Nova Scotia, . He married HEATHER BOOMER. He married IRENE McISSAC

     Michael Harry Walker and Irene McIsaac had the following children:

284   i.   HARRY^7 WALKER.

285   ii.   CHARLES WALKER.

286   iii.   JEFFREY WALKER

~~~~~~~~~~~~~~~~~~~~~~~~~~~~

206   MARK IAN^6 WALKER (Elsie Leone^5 Scott, Myrtle Jane^4, George^3, Richard^2, William^1) was born on 17 July 1956 in Woodstock ON. He married CATHERINE ALLES.

Mark Ian Walker and Catherine Alles had the following child:

287   i.   MARK THOMAS ALLES^7 WALKER.

~~~~~~~~~~~~~~~~~~~~~~~~~~~~

207   ROBERT FREDERICK^6 McGREGOR (Martha Elizabeth^5 Scott, Myrtle Jane^4, George^3, Richard^2, William^1) was born on 04 Oct 1936. He married Dorothy Joan Toohey on 20 Apr 1957 in Woodstock ON. She was

born on 09 Aug 1939 in Woodstock ON.

Robert Frederick McGregor and Dorothy Joan Toohey had the following children:

288   i.   ROBERT FREDRICK[7] McGREGOR was born in Oct 1957.

289   ii.   MARTY STEPHEN McGREGOR was born on 19 Sep 1958.

290   iii.   JONI FRANCES McGREGOR was born on 10 Jan 1966 in Woodstock. She married David Seminara on 03 Jun 1988 in Woodstock ON

~~~~~~~~~~~~~~~~~~~~~~~~~~~~~~~~~~

208   JAMES ALLAN[6] McGREGOR (Martha Elizabeth[5] Scott, Myrtle Jane[4], George[3], Richard[2], William[1]) was born on 09 Jun 1937 in Woodstock ON. He married Gabriel Lesley Knight on 07 Jun 1958 in Woodstock ON. She was born on 06 Jun 1942 in London, ON, .

James Allan McGregor and Gabriel Lesley Knight had the following children:

291   i.   JAMES VINCENT[7] MCGREGOR was born on 06 Nov 1958.

292   ii.   WENDY ELIZABETH KATHLEEN McGREGOR was born in Apr 1961.

293   iii.   VICTORIA LESLEY McGREGOR was born on 11 Nov 1965.

~~~~~~~~~~~~~~~~~~~~~~~~~~~~~~~~~~

209   BONNIE ELIZABETH[6] McGREGOR (Martha Elizabeth[5] Scott, Myrtle Jane[4], George[3], Richard[2], William[1]) was born on 13 Dec 1941 in Woodstock ON. She married (1) GARY RICHARD GEILING on 11 Jun 1958 in Woodstock ON. She married (2) JOHN FREDRICK WILFORD on 09 Feb 1971 in Woodstock ON. He was born on 29 Jan 1934. He died on 08

Oct 1989 in Woodstock ON.

Gary Richard Geiling and Bonnie Elizabeth McGREGOR had the following children:

294   i.   SANDRA LYNN[7] GEILING was born on 04 Dec 1959 in Woodstock ON. She married Rick Mure on 04 Dec 1983 in U.S.A..

295   ii.   MICHAEL CHARLES GEILING was born on 17 Jul 1960.

296   iii.   SUSAN PATRICIA GEILING was born on 21 Dec 1961 in Woodstock ON. She married DONALD LONGTIN.

John Fredrick Wilford and Bonnie Elizabeth McGREGOR had the following child:

297   i.   JENNIFER ELIZABETH[7] WILFORD was born on 29 Mar 1972 in Woodstock ON. She married Brad Vink on 21 Aug 1993 in Woodstock ON.

~~~~~~~~~~~~~~~~~~~~~~~~~~~~

210   MARLENE ANN[6] McGREGOR (Martha Elizabeth[5] Scott, Myrtle Jane[4], George[3], Richard[2], William[1]) was born on 20 Jul 1943 in Woodstock ON. She married John William McClellan on 26 Feb 1965 in Woodstock ON. He was born on 12 Jun 1933.

John William McClellan and Marlene Ann McGREGOR had the following children:

298   i.   JOHN CHRISTOPHER[7] McCLELLAN was born on 27 Oct 1965. He died on 19 Jul 1968 in Oxford co ON.

299   ii.   MERRITT ALLISON McCLELLAN was born on 31 Dec 1970.

300   iii. PAGE ELIZABETH McCLELLAN was born on 01 Mar 1973.

211   VIRGINIA JOYCE⁶ TOOHEY (Martha Elizabeth⁵ Scott, Myrtle Jane⁴, George³, Richard², William¹) was born on 08 May 1948 in Woodstock ON. She married JAMES WILLIAM BRIAN KENNEDY. He was born on 30 Dec 1942 in Bracebridge ON. He died on Oct3, 2013 in Huntsville ON .

James William Brian Kennedy and Virginia Joyce Toohey had the following children:

304   i.   DEBORA ELIZABETH⁷ KENNEDY was born on 08 May 1967.
306   ii.   JAMES FREDRICK KENNEDY was born on 05 Aug 1968.
307   iii. MATTHEW WILLIAM KENNEDY was born on 12 Apr 1973.

212   TIMOTHY LEWIS⁶ TOOHEY (Martha Elizabeth⁵ Scott, Myrtle Jane⁴, George³, Richard², William¹) was born on 09 Jan 1951 in Woodstock ON. He married Sandra May Foster on 22 Oct 1977 in Woodstock ON. She was born in Hamilton ON.

Timothy Lewis Toohey and Sandra May Foster had the following children:

308   i   GARY DAVID⁷ TOOHEY was born on 23 Sep 1979.
309   ii. CARLA ANN TOOHEY was born on 15 Jun 1982

213   KENNETH JAMES⁶ McINTYRE (Lauretta Abigail⁵ Parker, Edna Mae⁴, George³, Richard², William¹) was born on 20 Oct 1944 in Port Huron,

St Clair, Michigan, USA. He married Anita Grace Jordon on 11 Oct 1969 in St Clair, Michigan, USA. She was born Jan 1946 in Louisville, Jefferson, Kentucky, USA.

Kenneth James McIntyre and Anita Grace Jordon had the following children:

301   i.   ABIGAIL EVANS[7] McINTYRE was born on 20 Nov 1973.

302   ii.   JORDAN KENNETH McINTYRE was born on 18 Oct 1976.

214   PAUL DAVID[6] McINTYRE (Lauretta Abigail[5] Parker, Edna Mae[4], George[3], Richard[2], William[1]) was born on 03 Jun 1946 in Port Huron, St Clair, Michigan, USA. He married Maureen Ellen Russell on 14 Oct 1978 in Flint, Genesee, Michigan, USA. She was born Jul 1958 in Flint, Genesee, Michigan, USA.

Paul David McINTYRE and Maureen Ellen Russell had the following child:

303   i.   PAULA ELIZABETH[7] McINTYRE was born on 08 Jun 1981.

222   THOMAS RALPH[6] PARKER (Ralph Budd[5], Edna Mae[4], George[3], Richard[2], William[1]) was born on 08 Aug 1941 in Ingersoll ON . He married Ruth Anne Wailes on 09 Nov 1963 in Ingersoll ON . She was born on 24 Nov 1944 in London ON.

Thomas Ralph Parker and Ruth Anne Wailes had the following children:

310   i.   TERRANCE ALEXANDER[7] PARKER was born 25 Apr 1964.

311   ii.   KIMBERLEY ANNE PARKER was born on 13 Apr 1965.

312   iii. MICHAEL THOMAS PARKER was born on 24 Sep 1969.

313   iv. KRISTEN DAWN PARKER was born on 31 Jan 1974.

225   VIRGINIA GAYLE[6] PARKER (Ralph Budd[5], Edna Mae[4], George[3], Richard[2], William[1]) was born on 20 May 1954. She married SANDY BARTER.

      Sandy Barter and Virginia Gayle Parker had the following child:

314   i.   CONRAD JAMES[7] BARTER was born on 06 Jan 1987.

237   JAMES ALBERT FREDRICK[6] TOWN (Myrna Margaret Gail[5], Albert Lorne[4], George[3], Richard[2], William[1]) was born on 22 Nov 1957. He married Gloria Ann Raycroft on 06 Aug 1977 in Paris ON. She was born on 05 Jun 1959 in Paris ON.

      James Albert Fredrick Town and Gloria Ann Raycroft had the following children:

315   i.   COLIN JAMES[7] TOWN was born on 02 Mar 1980.

316   ii. BEVERLEY ANN TOWN was born on 19 Apr 1982.

333.   SHARON ELLEN MARIE TOWN ((Myrna Margaret Gail[5], Albert Lorne[4], George[3], Richard[2], William[1]) was born Dec 15, 1958 in Paris ON.

334.   CATHERINE LEE ANN TOWN (Myrna Margaret Gail[5], Albert Lorne[4], George[3], Richard[2], William[1]) born Nov 3, 1962. Married ROBERT JAMES COOMBS April 22, 1983. He was born Dec 12, 1962 in Oakville ON.

      Their children are:

335   i. ROBERT REGINALD JAMES COOMBS born June 3 1985 in Brantford ON.

336   ii. MATHEW ROBERT COOMBS born April 16, 1987 in Brantford

337   LORI LYNN TOWN (Myrna Margaret Gail[5], Albert Lorne[4], George[3], Richard[2], William[1]) was born Jaqn 18, 1964 Paris ON. Married WAYNE PEART July 23, 1983. He was born Oct 21, 1961 in Paris

    Their children are:

    i.   JASON WAYNE PEART born Nov 29, 1987 in Brantford

    ii. ADAM JAMES PEART born Sept 27, 1994 in Brantford

317   JANET ELAINE SELDON (Doris[5] Wallace [4], William, Richard, William) born Aug 24 1944 married Clive Tompkins born may 4 1942, married May 30 1970

    Their children are:

321   i   STEPHANIE CHRISTINE TOMPKINS born Aug 25 1974

322   ii JENNIFER ROBINS TOMPINS bornMay 16 1978

318   RUTH ELIZABETH SELDON born April 10 1946, married (1) Jack Laverne Hutson June 5, 1965 married (2) Bruce Wayne Flood Dec 15 1978

    Their children are:

322   I   TRACEY MAUREEN HUTSON born July 2 1967

323   ii SHANNON DEANNE HUTSON born July 12 1972

319   LINDA MARIANNE SELDON born 11 Dec 1950, married Aug 1 1970 to Gary John McLay born April 14 1951 live at 126 Innes St. Ingersoll

    Their children are:

324   i   TRAY CHRISTOPHER McCLAY born March 2 , 1972

325   ii RYAN DAVID McCLAY born Aug 18 1976

320   ROBERT GEORGE SELDON born Jan 11, 1953 married Susan Kathleen Kimberley born May 7 1952. Farm at RR 3 Ingersoll.

Their children:

326   i.   KIMBERLEY   REBECCA SELDON born 29 Oct 1978

327   ii   RICHARD WARREN SELDON born 8 Dec 1980

The Martindale Family Story

The name Martindale comes from the settlement of Martindale in the county of Westmorland (now part of Cumbria). The surname Martindale belongs to the large category of Anglo-Saxon habitation names which are derived from pre-existing names for towns, villages, parishes or farmsteads.

Early Origins of the Martindale family

Martindale is the name of an old Cumberland family dating back to the 14th century. The family held much property in that shire up to the 17th century and even later. An ecclesiastical district in Westmorland describes it this way. " The valley of Martindale lies close to Hawes Water in the Lake District of England. The valley is accessed across Deepdale Beck from Patterdale which is eight miles from Ambleside. The chapelry of Martindale has remained small over the centuries having only 198 people by the late 1800s. Many of the family were found in Yorkshire in the 15th century. The Corpus Christi Guild (Surtees Society) listed Katerina Martyngdale in 1475 and John Markyngdale in 1476."

Martindale valley is situated in the Lake District National Park. As of 2011 there were just about 100 people that lived within the parish. One of the oldest churches in the area, St. Martin's Church, is located in the Martindale valley.

People bearing the Martindale name have strong connections with Lancashire and Yorkshire where the name was most common in centuries past. Among the centers where Martindales have migrated are USA, Canada, Barbados.

An early Martindale was :
Martindale, Adam (1623–1686), a presbyterian leader, fourth son of Henry Martindale, was born at High Heyes in the parish of Prescot, Lancashire about 16 Sept. 1623 (baptized on 21 Sept.) His father, originally a substantial yeoman and builder, lost his money by investing in a friend's bad scheme. Adam became a minister and his writings landed him in trouble with the authorities during the civil war. He was a non conformist preacher. He had several children but no male heirs survived him.

This Martindale is likely a more direct ancestor but how is not known. **John Martindale** and his family lived at Dalton (Upholland) in the 1700's and are buried at St. Thomas the Martyr Church. John worked as a slater with the slate quarry. This same church is associated with the Fairhurst family.

The Known Family Tree

The next Martindale is even more closely related but the proof is not clear. **William Martindale**, father of Henry, was part of a family of Martindale or Martendale who lived in two small adjacent villages west of Wigan called Upholland and Dalton. William had a brother Thomas and their father was likely either Thomas or James and his mother Elizabeth. These people were stone masons. It is difficult to say exactly which William is referenced or even if we have the right connection to Henry.

So now we go into the speculation phase of who is who. It must be recalled that people tended to have a problem giving their correct ages.

In 1871 the year before he married Margaret a Henry Martindale (1842) was living at Upholland with his father Thomas age 63, mother Ann 69 and sister Mary 22. These men were both stone masons. This Thomas in 1851 was 46 and born like William at Dalton(Upholland), Ann was 40, son Henry was 9 (1842) , brother Thomas 18 and sister Mary 2. Ten years back in 1841 Thomas was 35, Ann 40, Elizabeth was 12 Thomas 9 and Henry was new born at the census. They were living on School lane Wigan. These facts fit except Henry reported his father as William but he could have been William Henry or Henry William.

So how does that fit for William? In 1802 on 7 Nov William son of Thomas Martendale (not i) was christened at Upholland. In 1803 on April 10 William son of James Martendale was also christened at Upholland. Later in 1851 this William was living with his wife Sarah and his mother Elizabeth at Kirkdale and in 1861 he and Sarah were still there. Or he might have actually been, according to the 1851 census, William born 1807, age 44 at Dalton (Upholland) whose wife was Betty age 45 and whose children were Henry age 13 (1838) and Hannah age 8.

Finally we have William in 1861 census born 1800 at Upholland living with his son John and Family at Upholland. Thus we have two Williams but the facts for Henry do not fit well. The village of Upholland's main industry was a stone and slate quarry dating to the 1300's which explains the family occupation trade.

Also these Williams have different fathers, Thomas and James, are presumably brothers. So it becomes too difficult to trace the family back past 1800.

Henry Martindale was born in the village of Upholland about 1843. His father was probably William. Henry was married twice because he was cited as widowed at the time of his marriage to the widow **Margaret Prescott**. His first wife was **Betsey Guffog** b. 1837. They were married in July of 1860 and she died in September 1870. Margaret Prescott was the daughter of Samuel Davies of Chorley and was born in July 1842 at St. Helen's. Margaret and Henry were married January 27, 1872 at Bolton le Moors, St. Peter. They had their children christened here as well. It is near her family home of Chorley and 8 miles south of Darwen. It is unlikely they attended this church regularly as it was some distance to travel as they lived for some years at 46 Highfield St., Over Darwen and also had lived for a time at Primrose Terrace, Darwen. At the time of his marriage and at other times until about 1890 he worked as a flagger, an occupation with an unclear definition perhaps directing horse drawn traffic with a flag at the mill. Later he worked as a mason a trade he may have also had earlier in life.

In the census of 1881 Henry and Margaret were living at Primrose Terrace on the edge of the India mills property where he may have been working. This was only a block or so from the Highfield house where he later lived and he was working as a stone cutter. Later he became weaver.

Cotton from India and America was the reason the India Mill was built during the 1860's. It was a large substantial building with 3 spinning floors, 2 carding floors and a blowing floor. Equipped with all the latest machinery and an imposing 300 Italian inspired tower it was to be a desirable place to work. Unfortunately it went broke resulting in the collapse of the cotton industry as a result of the American civil war. However by 1907 there were in Darwen and Over Darwen, home of the mill, more than 8,000 members in the Darwen Weavers Association. It was a major textile factory town and considered very progressive.

The children of Henry and Betsey were Mary Ellen Elizabeth born 1864 and Betsy born 1868 who married William Aspden b. 1866. Betsey died July 28, 1937. Mary Ellen Elizabeth known as Polly, as said, was born in 1864. She died in October 1930. She married Thomas James Kenyon born Aug 1861 on November 28 1885. He passed away in 1949.

The children of Henry and Margaret were William Henry who was born April 26, 1872 and presumably named after his grandfather and father, Martha Alice born 1874; John born April 22, 1875; Frederick born 1877 and Margaret Hannah baptized March 2, 1879 at Bolton le Moor. Samuel arrived in 1882 and Lillian was born in 1885. Lillian died age 18 in 1903 and is buried with her parents. Henry died age 66 at Darwen May 15, 1905. His wife Margaret Davies Prescott died in July 1915.

Henry Martindale   *Margaret Davies Prescott Martindale*

Samuel Martindale

Was born in Darwen, Lancashire, England in March of 1882. He was the youngest son of Henry Martindale(1843) and Margaret Davies Prescott (1842). Legend has it Henry was a stone mason who worked on sidewalks and stores.

In the census of 1891 we know that Henry was living on Highfield Street in Over Darwen and working as a flagger. Henry was 48 and Margaret was 50. Samuel was nine years old and shared the home with some of his siblings: William Henry 18, Martha Alice 17, John 16, Frederick 14 and Margaret 12.

In 1901 (Census) Samuel 19 was a cotton weaver at Darwen and his father Henry 58 was also a cotton weaver at Darwen. His brother Frederick (age 24) was working in Darwen as a stone mason. Another brother John was also working as a cotton weaver in Darwen. Other Martindales lived in the Wigan area.

Samuel married Elizabeth Fairhurst May 23 1907 and he was father to William Henry born Nov 2 1908 at 27 Frances St. Darwen, Margaret born July 18, 1910 and Gladys born April 10, 1917.

Samuel was grandfather of Donna and Brenda Phillips, Fred and Barry Crawford, and Karen Parkhill.

William Henry Martindale(Apr 26,1872) who remained in England married (Mary) Ellen Holden Jan 10 1899 at Darwen. She was the daughter of Renton Holden and was born in 1879. Mary Ellen died in 1930 but William Henry lived until 22 August 1949. Their child was Elsie.

William Henry Martindale   *Mary Ellen Holden*   *Elsie*

Samuel's brother, **John Martindale** born April 22 ,1875, was married to Agnes Adora Smith (born Nov 1877) on October 5, 1897 at Over Darwen. Her father was William Smith. John, like his father, was a stone mason and Agnes was a weaver. John and Agnes Dora with their daughter Doris born May 1903, and Lillian born Oct. 1897 emigrated to Brantford Ontario in 1910 and in 1911 they were living at 168 Murray St. Brantford and he was working at a wagon works as a laborer for 450 dollars a year. Agnes was caring for half a dozen lodgers. They were living there in 1921 when Doris was 18. Daughter Lillian was married to Harry Elliott and lived at 126 Mary Street, Brantford and then 55 Ontario Street where she also lived with her second husband Bill Davey. Lillian had a son Franklin Elliott. What became of Doris? Doris May Martindale daughter of John and Dora married William Clarence Davis whose mother was born in Minnesota USA on Dec 30 1922. Doris' family was living at 121 Mary St. Brantford. (More on John/Jack below.)

Frederick Martindale born 1877 (died 26th Feb. 1940) married Mary Harwood born 1875 on June 10, 1899. He emigrated to Brantford at the same time as John his brother. They landed at Quebec on board the Empress of

Ireland in 1910. In the census of 1911 he said he had arrived in 1899 but in fact the England Census of 1901 showed he was there age 24, Mary 25 and they had a newborn Norah. In the Canada census of 1911 his family consisted of Nora 11, Lillian 5 (born March 1906), and Gladys 2 (May 1908). All were born in England. They lived at # 32 Marlborough St, Brantford and he worked at "building" for $ 480.00 a year and worked 55 hours per week. Later they became Canadian citizens. On 4 April of 1920 Fred and his wife emigrated to Los Angeles California via Port Huron and stayed with John and Ellen Stingston (Stinchcomb?) of 2023 E. 27th St. Los Angeles with the intent of becoming residents. Frederick was described as 5 ft. 4 in tall with blue eyes and brown hair. He, Mary and girls remained there for a year and returnwd to Brantford in April 1921. Whether this had anything to do with Samuel's condition is not known. Fred's daughter Nora, born June 26 1900 in Darwen, married James Pollock and they moved to Minnesota. They had 2 boys Mark and ?. Nora died at Brainerd, MN on 23 April 1997. Fred's daughter Gladys married Cecil Edgar Pronger. She died in 2003 in Ocala, Florida. Their sons were Wayne and Gordon. Fred's Daughter Lillian married William Stevens. They had a son.

Fred's brother **John (Jack) Martindale** 1875, in 1922 also decided that he and his wife Agnes Dora would go to California and stay with Mrs. Ellen Stinchcomb also of 2023 E. 27th st. They entered at Port Huron October 22, 1922 and listed their daughter Lillian Elliott 126 Mary St, Brantford as kin. Lillian had married John Elliott 29 July 1919 in Brantford. Lillian's son was Franklin.

When John emigrated he was listed as 5ft 6inches tall, mostly bald brown hair and blue eyes, weight

136 lbs and occupied as a machinist. John soon relocated to Batavia N.Y. where he and Agnes settled. In 1926 John and Agnes Adora (Dora) became US citizens and he was a punch press operator living at 317 School St. Batavia. Meanwhile Fred decided to again return to the USA at age 45. He reported alone to Buffalo NY on August 3, 1924. He was now 5'3" tall with green eyes and was a Canadian citizen who lived at 108 Pearl St. Brantford where his wife remained. He intended to go and stay with his brother John at 174 Fitzhenry St South in Batavia. Fred was debarred entry because he had no visa. The reasons for not being given a visa were not explained. Fred returned to Pearl St. Brantford. Meanwhile John in 1930 was living in Batavia working as a press hand in a farm implement factory. He was 53 and Agnes 49. John may have died south of Buffalo in 1933 at North Collins NY. *(Photo of Jack and Agnes at Brantford)*

Samuel's sister **Martha Alice** (born 1873) remained in Darwen and married Benjamin Duncanson (Dunkenson) 16 April 1898 and lived at 12 Hodgson St. Darwen. Their children were Margaret who married 1. A Wood, 2. A Waring. Her children were Jim, Brian, Collin; Albert; then Harry who married and had daughters Valerie and Pauline; and Harold who married Martha ? and whose children were Bernard who married Sheila and had a son Andrew.

Martha Alice Martindale Duncanson &Albert Duncanson

Benjamin Duncanson

Harry   Harold

Duncanson

Lastly, **Margaret Hanna Martindale** (1879) married Walter Yates and their son was Stanley.

Walter Yates

Margaret Hannah

Elizabeth Fairhurst, Sam's wife, was born Feb 4,1884 at Hindley Green, a suburb of Wigan which is NW of Manchester. Darwen is North of Manchester. Elizabeth was the daughter of William Fairhurst and Margaret Birchall.

Samuel, it was reported, could play the organ and wished to earn a living as a piano teacher. However in 1911 he was living in Darwen working as a weaver.

~~~~~~~~~~~~~~~~~~~~

Darwen had more than 2 dozen weaving mills with more than 20, 000 looms. Most of the mills specialized in making cloth for sale to India and China. Samuel would have been familiar with terms like shirting, jaconettes (bandage cloth), dhooties (loincloth worn by men in India), sateens, twills, madapolems (soft fine yarn cotton). By 1907 the Darwen Weavers', Winders' and Warpers' Association had more than 8,000 members in a town of 30 000 people.

Much of Darwen was built between about 1850 and 1900. It was one of the first places in the world to have steam trams. The arrangement of town hall, market, public transport, eating/hotel facilities and the pre-suburban mixed-size vernacular housing, with local variations according to topography, is very characteristic of Northern England. The year 1900 perhaps represents the peak of Victorian optimism in the area.

Dr Andrew Gritt, director of the Institute of Local and Family History at the University of Lancashire writing about life in Darwen in 1911 said : "It is too easy to see life in industrial Lancashire as being grim, poor, dirty, and tough. For some it undoubtedly was, but large numbers of Lancastrians lived decent, if modest, lives."

Literacy was generally high amongst local people, in excess of 85 per cent in some areas.

Dr Gritt added: "Although this enabled self-improvement and adult education for some, the public house and the consumption of alcohol was a perceived social problem."

Dr Gritt says houses were usually small terraces and many of them still survive today which suggests that they were clearly not slums.

"The wages of textile workers were sufficient to enable many to have an annual holiday in Blackpool and outdoor leisure pursuits such as rambling and hill walking were extremely popular amongst the working class," he added.

The children of Darwen could expect to go to school until age 12 then enter the mills as half time workers with the other half of their day at school. That ended in 1920 when child labor was abolished.

~~~~~~~~~~~~~~~~~~~~~~~~~~~~

Samuel and Elizabeth were married 23 May 1907 and had William in 1908 and Margaret in 1910. In 1915, at the age of 33 Samuel decided to emigrate to Canada. His brothers John and Fred had already emigrated and must have sent back some favorable information about life in Canada. Samuel gave up his job in the mill and went to Canada where they stayed with his brother John in Brantford, ON. However the next year the family returned to England. What Samuel's reasons were we do not know. En route Elizabeth apparently conceived their youngest child Gladys who was born in England in April 1917.

Now for reasons which are totally unclear, Samuel enlisted in the army. He may have done this to avoid conscription because under the Military Service act of 1916 married men up to the age of 41 could be called for service. These people would have no options so joining up allowed a man to become a medic or hold another position. He was 35 years of age and had a young family. There could have been ample work in either Canada or England in those days. The war had been going on for over 3 years and the situation was not good. So what motivated him to sign up on August 20, 1917 is not clear but he may have in fact been conscripted or feared he would be. In addition he signed up as a medic which was where religious conscientious objectors were often placed.

He reported to Blackburn, the city next to Darwen, on Aug 30, 1917. His occupation was listed as a weaver, age 35 years. This was old for a soldier but for over a year men his age were being called up. His wife Elizabeth and children Gladys April 10 1917, Margaret July 18, 1910 and William 2 Nov 1908 were all at home at 27 Francis St. Darwen. This was a limestone row house next to a corner with an alley in the back. There was no lawn or play area as the house was right on the street. Margaret and William would have no outside play area except the street and the house had one window on the first and second floor facing the street. There was a second window on the back upstairs. An enclosed room at the back had a door to the alley but no windows. It may have been some sort of storage area, scullery and likely in the back a toilet. The window room was the parlor, behind it the kitchen/eating area and two bedrooms without closets were upstairs. Such was the rented terrace of Elizabeth and the children.

The street would have been used by cars, lorries, horses and people. People often held street parties to socialize with the neighbors and children did play on the streets. Unlike today the streets were not the preserve of the automobile which was as yet not common. It is not known if the house had indoor plumbing or whether the water came from a community source in the neighborhood. From the upstairs windows the open countryside could be seen. It was unlikely Elizabeth was working at this time as Gladys was an infant. Elizabeth was also a weaver.

Samuel was assigned service number 124741. For the next 142 days he was in training in England with the Royal Army Medical Corps. His training dealt with his role as an unarmed stretcher bearer and first aid assistant and hospital orderly. On the 8th day of January 1918 he was shipped to France and left Southampton bound for Le Havre. He joined the Cyclists Base Depot at Rouen on Jan 13 1918 as an ambulance cycle carrier. They were extensively used during the war. The cyclist would go forward with a stretcher attached to his cycle, link up with a second cyclist with the stretcher hooked between the two cycles and carry the injured back for treatment.

The work of a stretcher bearer:

"A man's chances of survival depended on how quickly his wound was treated; modern warfare was now producing vast numbers of casualties requiring treatment at the same time. Medical treated was to start as soon as feasible, and as near to the front line as possible, for this reason Regimental Aid Posts were set up. The Battalion Medical Officer, his orderlies and stretcher-bearers, attended these. In action, the RAP was situated a few metres behind the front line, this could have been in a dugout, in a communication trench, a ruined house, or a deep shell hole. The RMO had the same staff. The facilities were only sufficient to carry out first aid. The Regimental Aid Post had no holding capacity. Wounded men were to either make their own way or be carried, usually by a member of his own Unit. The object of the exercise was to patch them up and either return them to their duties in the line or pass them back, via hand carriage, wheeled stretchers,

or walk if he was able to, to an Advance Dressing station. Those who were in need of further treatment were collected by RAMC Stretcher Bearers from the Advanced Dressing Station and taken to the ADS. There were teams of RAMC stretcher bearers, strung out over miles of ground unpassable by motor or horsed transport, that shuttled between the posts and passing the wounded on to the next team. A 'carry' could be anything up to four miles over muddy or shell-pocked ground, either in trenches or above ground."

The next day January 14, 1918 Samuel was posted to Wimereux Base Hospital. In the First World War, Boulogne and Wimereux formed an important hospital center and until June 1918 the medical units used Wimereux Communal Cemetery for burials. Colonel John McCrae, the gunner and doctor who wrote the popular war poem "In Flanders Fields", served and died in the hospital and is buried here.

The Base Hospital was part of the casualty evacuation chain, further back from the front line than the Casualty Clearing Stations. They were manned by troops of the Royal Army Medical Corps, with attached Royal Engineers and men of the Army Service Corps. In the theatre of war in France and Flanders, the British hospitals were generally located near the coast. They needed to be close to a railway line in order for casualties to arrive (although some also came by canal barge). They also needed to be near a port where men could be evacuated for longer-term treatment in Britain.

There were two types of Base Hospital, known as Stationary and General Hospitals. They were large facilities, often centered on some pre-war buildings such as seaside hotels. The hospitals grew hugely in number and scale throughout the war. Most of the hospitals moved very rarely until the larger movements of the armies in 1918. Some hospitals moved into the

Rhine bridgehead in Germany and many were operating in France well into 1919. Most hospitals were assisted by voluntary organizations, most notably the British Red Cross.

Things did not go well for Samuel for less than a week into his posting at Wimereux he was hauled up on Jan 22 for being disrespectful to an officer. Then a couple of weeks after that he was given 7 days in detention for irregular conduct. In March he was again hauled up for wilfully idling his time. And then in April he was given 3 more days for being dirty on parade. Whether all of this was symptomatic of his larger problems or his discontent with the military is not known.

He was posted to # 61 service squadron at Dieppe on Aug 8, 1918 so apparently from May to August he was not in any more trouble. However after only a few days at Dieppe he was reprimanded for absenting himself from convoy duty between 6:30 pm and 9:30 pm on August 16. That was followed up by being disrespectful to a warrant officer on September 14, 1918.

At the end of the war he was given a 14 day leave and allowance to return to England. So from Dec 29, 1918 to January 18, 1919 he was able to see his family. However he got sick and was admitted to hospital for bronchitis, or possibly the Spanish flu, when he reported back for duty. On Feb 1, 1919 he was again shipped back to England and sent to army headquarters at Aldershot.

His service with the British Expeditionary force was from Jan 9 1918 to Feb 30 1919. After that he was with the European Expeditionary Force from 15 April 1919 to 20 September 1919, 141 days.

On the 21 March 1919 he was assigned to the hospital ship "Gascon" and departed the 5th of April for Al Qantarah El Sharqiyya a northeastern Egyptian city on the eastern side of the Suez Canal. They arrived in May. The Gascon was a hospital ship that transported the injured from battlefields such as the Gallipoli battlefield to Egypt. There was a major war hospital at this town and beside it a major war cemetery, The Kantara Commonwealth War Graves Commission Cemetery and Memorial. The cemetery was begun in February 1916 and was in use until late 1920. The Kantara hospital took in the survivors of the Gallipoi battles and those injured in fighting in Jordan. A great many died as the adjacent cemetery shows.

Samuel was posted to work at this hospital that by now was dealing only with the most severe survival cases. He worked there from May to August 1919. Samuel lost it in Egypt. He had a severe mental breakdown. We don't know how or why. On the 19th of August 1919 he was placed on disability and shortly sent to Cardiff Wales for mental treatment. This was the first establishment, recently set up, to deal with post traumatic stress disorder.

By the end of World War One the army had dealt with 80,000 cases of 'shell shock'. As early as 1917 it was recognized that war neuroses accounted for one-seventh of all personnel discharged for disabilities from the British Army. Once wounds were excluded, emotional disorders were responsible for one-third of all discharges. Even more worrying was the fact that a higher proportion of officers were suffering in this way. According to one survey published in 1917, while the ratio of officers to men at the front was 1:30, among patients in hospitals specializing in war neuroses, the ratio of officers to men was 1:6. What medical officers quickly realized was that everyone had a 'breaking point', weak or strong, courageous or cowardly - war frightened everyone witless.

At the Cardiff Hospital Britain had established an early effort to treat those affected by PTSD or shell shock. Samuel was admitted. He was diagnosed with hallucinations and aggressive behavior. He was judged to be 20% functional, a condition that was presumed likely to last six months. He was awarded a pension or weekly gratuity of 1 pound 28 shillings for the upkeep of his family.

On the 12th of July 1920, having been there since the previous summer, he was released from the hospital. The authorities said his aggravation had passed away and there were no grounds for further awards. The pension expired. His condition was assessed that he was 70% functional. He was judged dull and retarded and "does simple calculations with difficulty." Essentially he now knew his name and could count to 10 so he was cured.

Two weeks later July 26th 1920 he was discharged from the army as being no longer physically fit. He was given the medal of victory (RAMC/101Bq8, Page 7502) which all veterans received. The fact that he had previously been accepted into the medical cops as able and fit was of no matter. He was no longer enlisted and not needing a disability pension.

Back with his family, it was decided to return to Canada. Apparently he had come into a little money or had some savings or help so the trip was affordable.

In late 1920 Samuel again returned to Canada and Brantford. Fred and his wife Mary (Harwood) (AKA Polly) also emigrated in 1910 and lived at 108 Pearl Street Brantford with their daughters Lillian 15 and Gladys 12. Fred was listed as a laborer. John having been in Canada for 11years was earning 1125 dollars a year as a press hand and living at 20 Glanville Ave Brantford.

John was 47 (born 1875) and Agnes Adora (Smith) 44 (1878). They eventually moved to the USA. Fred remained in Brantford.

Samuel had a great deal of difficulty adjusting to civilian life. In 1921 he was 39 years old and living on East Broadway in Paris. Elizabeth was 36 and Bill was 12, Margaret 10 and Gladys 4. The older children were in school. Sam could not sleep, had bad dreams, and was in no way cured of his problems. Elizabeth sought help from a mental hospital in Hamilton. She was told since he was a British war veteran he would be eligible for treatment in England if he went back. Apparently Canada was not prepared to care for him.

So approximately 1925 -26 Gladys went with her mother to the hospital in Hamilton to give her father a bundle of clothes and say goodbye to him. Apparently the other 2 children were now working as they were over 14. They did not go to say goodbye. None of his family ever saw him again although he lived until September 1953. He was buried on October 2nd 1953 in Darwen. He spent the rest of his life at Queen's Park Hospital/workhouse in Blackburn, Lancashire. He was admitted by himself each time. He first was admitted on the 28 of August 1926. After he arrived from Canada, he went to stay with his sister Martha Duncanson of 12 Hodgson St. Darwen who was his contact person as next of kin. His admission number was 4173 and his occupation was listed as weaver. After a few months he was discharged on February 22, 1927 but 4 days later readmitted himself. He left again on March 10, 1927 but was back the next day. After a couple of months he again left for one day May 24, 1927 but was back the next day and stayed for nearly a month before leaving June 21, 1927. Two days later June 23, 1927 he readmitted himself and never again had a record that he left. We can only guess at why he left. Possibly to deal with some personal matters and possibly he realized he could not manage on his own.

The Blackburn Union Workhouse was built in 1864 for 1000 inmates. It was built to house the poor. It became the Queen's Park Hospital basically after 1948 but earlier in the century it had been a multipurpose institution for orphans, the poor, mentally troubled, and indigent people. It was to its care he admitted himself. It was believed that he was there under the care of a military scheme but there is no evidence of this. He was a ward of the state in a poor house. The inmates of the institution had some benefits. An on site cinema and a bowling green were created for the inmates. His pension or veteran's care are not known. Neither is it known that as an inmate, was he able to use his training as a medic and thus have been useful.

He spent the rest of his life, nearly 30 years, in an institution. Elizabeth sent him money from time to time to help him out although some family felt he had no need of this.

Until Gladys, when she was over 90 years old, told her niece, Donna, the story of how he came to return to England, it was thought that Sam had chosen to go back. It was a family secret that he had been sent back for treatment and care. Samuel Martindale died September 23, 1953 and was buried October 2nd with his parents at "Blackburn with Darwen Unitary Authority", Darwen Cemetery.

Elizabeth Fairhurst Martindale, his wife, died 1975 in Paris, Ontario.

Inscription

In loving memory of Henry, the beloved husband of Margaret Martindale who died May 15th 1905, Aged 66 years. Also Margaret, Wife of the above who died Aug 25th 1915, Aged 74 years. Also of Lilian, their daughter who died Feb 26th 1905, Aged 20 years. Also Samuel their son, who died Sept 28th 1953, Aged 73 years..... Tombstone at Darwen.

The Fairhurst Family

The Fairhurst Name comes from the English county of Lancashire and is a habitational name from a hamlet near Parbold, not far from Wigan, so named from Old English fæger 'beautiful' + hyrst 'wooded hill'.

Elizabeth Fairhust 1884/1975 was the middle child of William and Margaret Fairhurst. She married Samuel Martindale.

Several Fairhurst families were in the Wigan area as early as 1600 and early records of the name mention Henry de FAIRHURST, 1260, County Lancashire, but we will begin our exploration with the census of 1891 on Alder Lane, Hindley Lancashire. Today Alder lane has only a couple of buildings that could have been there in 1891. One side of the road is meadow and golf course, the other is a street of fairly new houses with only a couple of exceptions. So likely they lived in a semi rural location. Here on Alder lane Elizabeth Fairhurst was six years old living with her family. William Fairhurst her father was 36, born 1855, and was working as a coal miner. Margaret his wife was 34, born 1857. At home were Harriot (Harriet) 11, William Edward 9, Elizabeth 6, Joseph 5, and Alice 1. Alice on two different census records 1891 and 1901 both state that she had been born in the USA. There is no explanation for this. Elizabeth recalled her father working as a fireman perhaps as part of his work as a miner.

First we shall go back to the 1881 census, then go to the 1901 in order to understand the situation.

In 1881, Margaret (Birchall) Fairhurst, was identified as married, mother of Harriet a newborn, and was living on Woodhill street, Elton, Lancashire with her 14 year old sister Hanna Fairhurst. Mother and sister had been born in Liverpool while Harriet had been born at Hindley Green. There is no mention of William because Margaret was identified as head of the family and her occupation was that of cotton warper. This information does not identify her maiden name. William at the time age 26 was in Hindley visiting James Hopkins where he was identified as married and working as a coal miner.

According to the England register they had been married in the spring of 1877 at Bury, Lancashire.

In 1901 Harriet age 20 was living with her uncle Joseph Lomax of Bolton now in Darwen. Lomax age 54, was an engine tenter. Lomax's wife was Margaret's older sister Elizabeth. Elizabeth Fairhurst, 16, was living with her father and his second wife Betsey. Sometime between 1891 and 1901 Margaret, Elizabeth's mother, had died and Elizabeth recalls not much liking her stepmother Betsey. A Margaret Fairhust died at Wigan 1893. Betsey was 46 and had been born at Oswaldtwistle. William now working as a blacksmith's striker had been born at Whiston Lancashire. Elizabeth was now 16 and working as a cotton weaver. Joseph 14, like Elizabeth born at Hindley Green, was working as a winder up at a paper mill. Alice was at school, age 11, and inexplicably, identified as having been born in America. The family was now living in Darwen.

By 1911 William and Betsey,(now Betty), along with her older sister were still in Darwen and he was working as a cotton weaver. The children had all departed. William died in January 1932 and was reported to have had two more wives after Margaret and Betsy.

According to the research of Dene Matheson Schiefer in 2020 William born 1855 in Whiston Lancashire was the son of Edward Fairhurst 1827-1876 and Jane Forshaw born 1821 who were married April 13, 1851 at St. Helen's Lancashire. Jane Forshaw was daughter of Joseph Foreshaw and Alice Jenkins. Joseph was the son of Thomas Forshaw and Isabel who were from West Denby. In turn Edward Fairhurst was the son of John Fairhurst and Mary Ann.

Margaret Birchall, William's first wife, was born Feb 4, 1856. They had 12 children of whom 5 lived. Margaret died at the age of 38 in 1893. Her living children were Harriet 1880, William (Bill) 1882 who fought in the Boer war, Elizabeth 1885 who married Sam Martindale, Joseph (Joe) 1886, Alice 1890.

Margaret's father was **John Birchall,** who was 42 in 1861 and was living at Kirkdale, a suburb of Liverpool near the docks. The family lived at the factory cottages. John was employed as a sadler. He was born in Preston. His wife Harriet also 42 was from Wolverhampton. The children: Elizabeth 15 was born in Staffordshire at Wednesbury and later married Joe Lomax. Samuel 11, Margaret 5, and John 3 were all born at Liverpool. Margaret was born 30 January 1856 and christened April 4th. Her mother was recorded as Margaret and father as John.

In 1871, John and Harriet and sons Samuel and John were living at Everton, a few blocks from Kirkdale, where he was still a saddler, but Margaret was now living with the Lomax family in Darwen. She was 15 and working as a cotton winder. The cotton mills of Darwen were attracting workers at this time. How she met William is not known.

Margaret Birchall married **William Fairhurst** at Bury, a village west of Bolton in 1877. Their children were:

Harriet Fairhurst 1880, married Jack Howard and their children were: Allen, William, Jack, Charlie, Alice.

Bill Fairhust 1882, married 1. Sybil, 2. Mary and their children were: Margaret (Peggy), Sybil, Alice, Joe, Edward, Jim, and William. Bill signed up with the British army around 1899/1900 to participate in the 2nd Boer War in South Africa. His photos show he had 6 medals, one for service under Victoria and one for service under Edward. The others cannot be determined.

(Bill and Sybil about 1902)

In the 1950's Bill and his wife Mary came to Paris Ontario to visit his sister Elizabeth Martindale whom he had not seen since 1920. This event resulted in a news item in the local paper.

Alice Fairhurst 1890, married Jim Shuttleworth. No children.

Shuttleworth

Elizabeth Fairhurst 1885, married Sam Martindale

Joe Fairhurst 1886, married Agnes ? And their children were: Margaret and Joe who was killed in the war.

Bill Martindale, Bill and Mary Fairhurst, and sister Elizabeth Martindale, and her daughter Margaret Phillips at Niagara Falls about 1958

Elizabeth Fairhurst born Feb 4 1884 at Hindley Green near Wigin met **Samuel Martindale** born March 1882 presumably while they were working at the cotton mills in Darwen. In Canada Elizabeth lived at Paris and worked at Wincey Mills where she operated an old style loom as a weaver until she was about age 72. She never lost her accent and delighted in singing music hall songs from England. She lived on her own after Samuel went back to England until just before she died. While she sent him parcels, there are no known letters back. At New Years Eve she would down her drink in one gulp. Elizabeth was a spiritualist and believed she was visited by deceased relatives and others. At her funeral the spiritualist leader called for the spirits to come into the room to carry her away. She was buried in the same grave as her son at Paris Ontario where she died in 1975. Their children were:

William (Bill), Margaret, Gladys

Margaret Martindale born July 18, 1910. She married Donald Truman Phillips at Paris Ontario October 7, 1939. Their stories are in the Phillips family story section pages 78,79. Their daughters were Brenda Elizabeth who married John Clausen and Donna Margaret who married John Eacott.

Gladys Martindale born April 17, 1917 married Ken Crawford b. 1914 of Woodstock a member of a family involved in Crawford Cartage in Woodstock. They were introduced by Don Phillips and married in 1939. Ken enlisted in the army during the second world war. Of the 3 children Gladys was the only one to go to the 10th grade and her brother was upset that she did not go on to complete her high school. He felt that he and his sister were working so she could keep going to school whereas they could not. This was a point of contention all of their lives. Their children were Barry born Oct 15, 1939 who married Audrey Bakker and later moved to Texas. They had a daughter Annette who had two

children. Fred, his brother, was born in 1947, never married and worked as a brick layer and stone mason. Gladys died Dec 31, 2010 at Woodstock, Ontario. She was sister in law of Dorothy Rohrer, Jean Crawford, Irene Crawford - Siano. Ken Crawford 1914 -1985 was son of Frederick James Crawford and Justina Christina Louise Wilkerson.

(*Photo Gladys & Barry*)

William Henry Martindale the oldest was born Nov 2 1908 at 27 Frances St. Darwen Lancashire. He married Mildred Irene Tucker born 1914 daughter of Gladys and John Tucker who had been farmers near Paris (on Keg Lane) but moved into Paris where John worked. William (Bill) worked at Penman's in Paris and lived on West River Street sharing a duplex with his mother before buying a house on Banfield St. He worked at Penman's his entire life from age 14 until he retired in his 70's. He had no pension and was presented with a watch at retirement. As he was a frugal person, he bought many saving bonds for his retirement. At one time his arm was caught in a loom at work and the upper arm was mangled and after that he never wore a short sleeve shirt . Bill spent many years as a loom repair fixer and when that section closed he worked as a dyer in the vats. They lost a daughter stillborn at birth Feb. 26 1934 who was buried with her maternal grandparents. Their next daughter Karen was born June 4 1950 and she married Sept 6, 1969 Rick Parkhill born Sept. 5 1950. Bill Martindale died Sept 10, 1998 and was buried at Paris. Mildred lived with her daughter until she died June 7, 2006 near Bracebridge ON.

Photo of Mildred and Bill

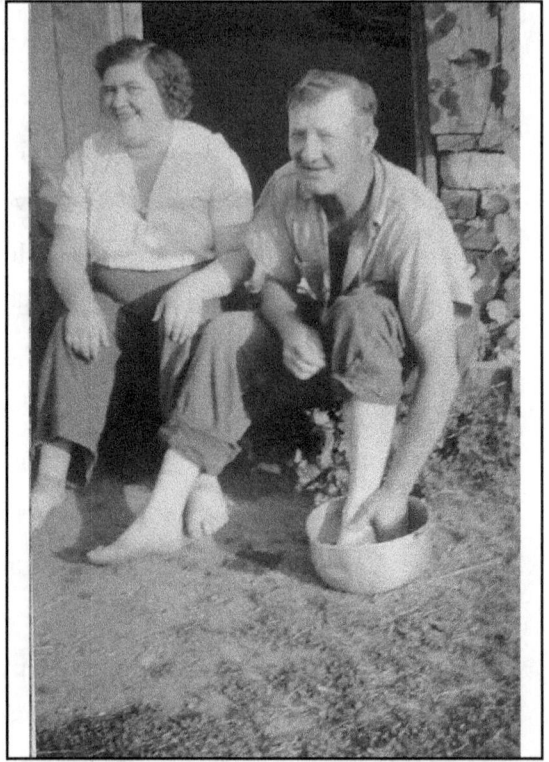

Mildred & her father
John Tucker

Karen and Rick Parkhill's children are: Tracie born Feb 27, 1970, who married Samuel Fasullo born Sept. 21, 1971 married Aug 21, 1999; Scott Parkhill b. April 14, 1974 married Tammy Sharpe on June 29, 2013; and Kevin Parkhill born March 5, 1977 married Stacey Kapek on Aug 11, 2001 divorced and then partnered with Jennifer Lafee.

Next Generation

Tracie Parkhill and Sam Fasullo's children are:

 i. Samuel Fasullo b. Oct 10, 2006

 ii. Nathan Fasullo b. April 27, 2009

 iii. Matthew Fasullo b. Sept. 9, 2010

   They live in British Columbia

Scott Parkhill's step children and Tammy Sharpe's children are

2 children and 3 grand children.

Kevin Parkhill and Stacey Kapek children are:

i.   Ryan b. Sept. 19, 1998

ii. Braeden b. March 7, 2005

iii. Vanessa b. Aug 7, 2008

iv. Cole   b. June 15, 2010

They divorced

Kevin Parkhill's step children and partner Jennifer Lafee's children are Kendra, Matthew, Morgan.

Penman's in the lives of the Martindale and Phillips families.

Elizabeth Fairhurst worked at the Wincey Mill and two of her children and a son in law all worked at Penman's in Paris. Starting in 1924 William Bill Martindale and later his sister Margaret became employees of this company. Later Don Phillips and his nephew Richardt were also employed there.

The Penman family came to Woodstock Ontario from NewYork in 1860 where they set up a textile mill. In 1897 they consolidated several smaller operations in a new factory in Paris Ontario. It became the largest employer in the small town. In 1906 it became Penman's Limited Company and set about expanding to a number of other towns and cities. The company made underwear, socks and other items of clothing. Like most textile companies they employed many men and women. Although they paid lower than average wages, the company was able to meet their payroll during the 1930's depression and not lay off workers. The company owned a number of houses which they rented to workers but also encouraged their employees to buy a home. The idea was to keep people from leaving for better pay in Brantford and other places. In the 1930's a sock fasterner was able to earn $16 a week and in the early 1940's during the war there were wage and price controls. The company encouraged piece work and faster workers could earn a lot more up to $50 a week. The company in response lowered the rate paid for piece work and that did not please the workers. Success of union organizers in Quebec and the Communist leanings of a couple of workers at the time led to efforts to bring in a textile union connected to the American Federation of Labor (AFL).

By 1949 the company had 2,700 employees and 650 were at the Paris factory. The average wage at the time across Ontario was $2000 per year and the textile workers averaged about $1800. Paris was not an expensive place to live and the majority of the workers, some with two income families, felt they had a comfortable middle class life style. The highest paid employees were the machine fixers who earned $3,400 a year which was much more than the $ 2,400 local high school teachers earned. Bill Martindale was employed as a fixer for most of his career.

The company, aware of the agitation for a union, proposed an independent company union. The deal offered was no strikes allowed and disputes would go to arbitration. The dues would be 25 cents a month. Decades earlier the company had negotiated with the employees to reduce the working hours by giving a 1 pm closing time on Saturday afternoon. The AFL organizers wanted dues of $2.50 a month, a closed shop, and more pay and shorter hours of work. The Labour Board of Ontario denied the company proposal and a vote was organized in late 1948. This created a great deal of stress in the entire town. The vote was very close as 329 out of 650 voted by 4 votes to join the union. The union presented their demands and the company said no. A strike was called for January 18th. It was cold mid winter and those who opposed the union as well as some who had voted for it refused to strike and continued to go to work. Bill Martindale crossed the picket line and was called scab. He had sugar put in his gas tank. When Don Phillips went to work in the beginning of the strike someone said, "You're not going in are you?" and convinced him to go home. As money got scarce and when he found out the people who had told him to go home were already back, he went back too. The OPP sent in more than 50 officers to protect the employees. The picket line was poorly supported and some reinforcements were sent in. Some of the women on the line, irritated by the police presence, took to using hat pins to poke the officers. One went to the hospital with an infection from one of these pokes. Quite a number of people were arrested in several skirmishes and spent time in the local jail. In the end only about 70 strikers supported the cause and on April 11 the strike was called off. Some strikers took other jobs but the company no longer had a strangle hold on the town and the company altered some of its practices. In 1965 Dominion Textiles bought the company and began to restructure. When Bill Martindale's job as a fixer ended, he went to work as a dyer in the vats. Don Phillips, who like Bill had worked at the #2 mill, operated wool carding machines in a very dusty environment. He left Penman's a few years after the strike and took a job managing a garage on Mill Street in Woodstock. Differences with the owner resulted in him leaving and taking another job before finding employment, through a friend, at a new company Fisher Controls where he assembled valves. He assisted his nephew Richardt ,who had been a sewing machine repairer, in also getting a job at Fisher Controls. Later he got his daughter Donna a summer job in the office of the same company.

Don's wife, Margaret Martindale, worked at Penman's from the age of 15 until her daughter Brenda was born in 1941. She said she would have liked to have continued at school but had to go to work for the family income. At one time she left the company and found work with a friend in Hamilton at the Chipman Holton Knitting Company which made hosiery. However Penman's valued her work ethic and she returned there where she fastened the cuff onto socks. Why she changed employers is not known. When Don and Margaret were married, the company offered them a house to rent. Margaret attempted to return to work but finally decided she would rather be a stay at home mother. Her mother Elizabeth worked at the Wincey Mills where she did weaving on old-fashioned looms. She used to weave the material for baseball uniforms in the era when they were grey with narrow stripes. She was at least 72 when she retired to live off the old age pension. Margaret returned to work in the shipping department of Harvey Woods on Mill Street in Woodstock after her children had grown up.

Bill, Gladys and   Mother Elizabeth Martindale about 1925

Margaret mother Elizabeth and Gladys Martindale around 1930

Martindale family about 1915 Grandma Margaret in center right of Betsey

Joe Fairhurst, who was brother of Elizabeth, died fighting in WW2.

Ken Crawford   *Don & Margaret Phillips & Family about 1950*
Husband of Gladys

Brenda, Aunt Myrtle Scott, Donna, Margaret Martindale Phillips

Donna and Brenda Phillips

This professional photograph was so well liked by the firm that took the picture that they featured a copy of it in their store front window in downtown Paris for a long time. Their Aunt Mildred saw it and went in a bought a copy for herself. It had been color tinted.

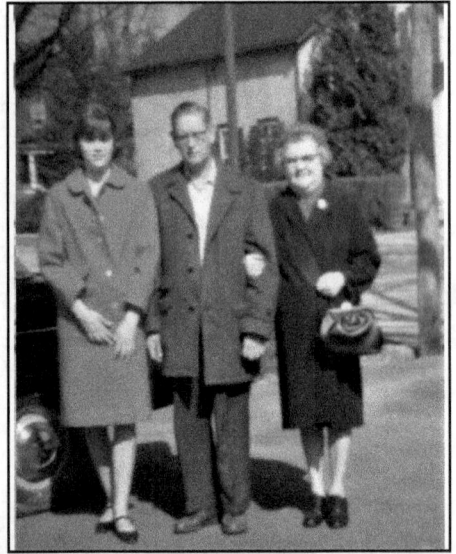

Bill, Mildred and Karen
Martindale Parkhill

Karen and Kelly Clausen, Margaret Phillips, Elizabeth Martindale at
Memorial drive Brantford Ont. About 1971

Brenda Clausen
Donna Eacott
2019

John and Donna
Eacott circa 2007